Trey Yingst

A Biography Book Narrating The Events Of
October 7th, The Saturday That Turned
Black

Robert Fox Johnson

Content

Dedication

To the memory of those lost on October 7th, 2023, and to the resilience of those who survived.

May their stories inspire us to seek understanding, to pursue truth, and to never lose hope for peace.

For journalists everywhere who risk their lives to bring light to the darkest corners of our world.

And for Trey Yingst, whose courage and compassion in the face of tragedy remind us of the power of bearing witness.

Preface

In the early hours of October 7th, 2023, the world watched in shock as a series of attacks unfolded across southern Israel. At the center of this maelstrom stood Trey Yingst, a young American journalist whose courage and dedication would soon be put to the ultimate test.

This book aims to tell two intertwined stories: that of Trey Yingst, a rising star in war correspondence, and the harrowing events of a day that would reshape the Middle East. Through Yingst's eyes, we witness not only the unfolding tragedy but also the raw human experiences that often get lost in the broad strokes of history.

As an author, I found myself drawn to Yingst's story not just for its connection to a momentous historical event, but for what it reveals about the nature of modern journalism. In an era of instant news and social media, Yingst represents a breed of reporters who still believe in the power of being there, of bearing witness, no matter the personal cost.

The events of October 7th are complex and emotionally charged. This book does not aim to pass judgment or take sides in the long-standing conflicts of the region. Instead, it seeks to provide a clear, factual account of what happened that day, while also exploring the human stories behind the headlines.

This book offers an intimate look at both the professional challenges and personal toll of reporting from conflict zones. It also examines the broader implications of the October 7th attacks, from their impact on regional stability to their influence on global politics.

Writing this book has been a sobering experience. It has reinforced my belief in the importance of quality journalism in our understanding of world events. It has also reminded me of the incredible resilience of the human spirit in the face of unimaginable adversity.

As you read, I invite you to consider not just the events described, but also the larger questions they raise about conflict, media, and our shared humanity. In the end, this is not just Trey Yingst's story, or even just the story of October 7th. It is a reflection on how we bear witness to history in the making, and what that witness costs us all.

Part I: Trey Yingst - The Making of a War Correspondent

1. Early Life and Formative Years

Trey Yingst's journey to becoming a renowned war correspondent began far from the conflict zones he would later cover. Born on September 10, 1993, in Harrisburg, Pennsylvania, Yingst grew up in a world that was about to be reshaped by the events of September 11, 2001. This timing would prove significant, as it meant that Yingst's formative years were shaped by a post-9/11 America, where foreign affairs and conflict reporting took center stage in the national consciousness. The Yingst family had deep roots in central Pennsylvania. Trey's father, Robert Yingst, worked as a respected attorney in the area, known for his dedication to his clients and his community. His mother, Deborah Yingst, was a teacher who instilled in her children a love for learning and a curiosity about the world beyond their immediate surroundings.

The family's ethos of service and engagement with the wider world had a profound impact on young Trey. Dinner table conversations often revolved around current events, with Robert and Deborah encouraging their children to form and express their own opinions.

This environment fostered Trey's early interest in world affairs and laid the groundwork for his future career. Trey was the middle child, with an older sister and a younger brother. Growing up, he was known for his energy, his inability to sit still, and his constant stream of questions. His sister, Lauren, often joked that Trey's future as a journalist was evident from an early age – he never stopped asking "why?"

Childhood in a Changing World

Trey's childhood coincided with a period of significant global change. The aftermath of 9/11, the wars in Afghanistan and Iraq, and the increasing globalization of media all played out during his formative years. While many of his peers might have found these events distant or abstract, Trey was captivated by them.

He would often be found glued to the television, watching news reports from far-flung corners of the world. The faces of reporters like Christiane Amanpour and Anderson Cooper became as familiar to him as those of cartoon characters were to other children his age. Trey was particularly drawn to war correspondents, fascinated by their bravery and their ability to bring distant conflicts into American living rooms. This fascination didn't always sit well with his parents, who worried about the impact of such heavy subject matter on a young mind. But they also recognized and respected Trey's genuine interest. Instead of discouraging him, they sought to channel his curiosity in productive ways.

For his tenth birthday, instead of the latest video game console that many of his friends were getting, Trey asked for a subscription to Time magazine. His parents, both amused and impressed by the request, obliged. From then on, Trey would eagerly await each new issue, poring over articles about world events and dreaming of one day seeing these places for himself.

School Days: The Budding Journalist

Trey's academic journey was marked by his growing passion for journalism and current affairs. At Lower Dauphin High School in Hummelstown,

Pennsylvania, he quickly became involved with the school newspaper, The Falcon Flash. Starting as a freshman reporter, Trey worked his way up to become the paper's editor-in-chief in his senior year.

His time at The Falcon Flash was transformative. Trey discovered he had a talent not just for writing, but for asking the right questions and for presenting complex information in a clear, engaging manner. He covered everything from school board meetings to local sports events, always pushing to find the most interesting angle on even the most mundane stories.

One of Trey's high school teachers, Mrs. Samantha Collins, remembers him as a student who stood out for his drive and his mature approach to journalism. "Most high school students see the school paper as a fun extracurricular activity," she recalls. "But Trey treated it like a professional job. He was always pushing for better stories, more in-depth reporting.

He wasn't content with just reporting what happened – he always wanted to know why it happened and what it meant."

It was during this time that Trey had his first taste of covering a major news event. In 2011, when he was a junior, central Pennsylvania was hit by severe flooding caused by the remnants of Tropical Storm Lee. While professional journalists descended on the area, Trey saw an opportunity to provide a local, youth perspective on the disaster.

He spent days wading through flooded streets, interviewing affected families, and documenting the community's response to the crisis. His series of articles for The Falcon Flash caught the attention of local media, and Trey found himself being interviewed by a Harrisburg television station about his reporting. This experience was a turning point for Trey. It confirmed his passion for journalism and gave him a glimpse of the impact that dedicated reporting could have. It also taught him valuable lessons about the challenges and responsibilities of covering traumatic events – lessons that would serve him well in his future career.

Beyond the Classroom

Trey's drive to understand the world wasn't limited to his academic pursuits. He was an avid participant in Model United Nations, where he honed his skills in research, public speaking, and diplomatic negotiation. These experiences further broadened his understanding of international relations and global politics.

In his spare time, Trey voraciously consumed books about journalism and world history. He was particularly inspired by works like "The Race for Timbuktu" by Frank T. Kryza, which recounted the 19th-century European exploration of Africa. Such books fueled his desire to someday report from far-flung and challenging environments. Trey also sought out opportunities to gain practical experience in journalism beyond the school newspaper. He interned at a local radio station during his junior year, learning the ropes of broadcast journalism. This experience opened his eyes to the power of the spoken word and the immediate impact of live reporting – skills that would prove invaluable in his future career.

The College Decision

As Trey approached the end of his high school years, the question of college loomed large. With his passion for journalism and international affairs firmly established, he set his sights on schools with strong programs in these areas.

After considering various options, Trey ultimately chose American University in Washington, D.C. The decision was influenced by several factors.

American University's School of Communication was well-regarded in the field of journalism. Moreover, the university's location in the nation's capital offered unparalleled opportunities for internships and networking in both journalism and international relations.

Trey's parents, while supportive, had some reservations about his chosen path. They worried about the challenges and dangers of a career in journalism, particularly given Trey's interest in conflict reporting. Robert Yingst recalls a conversation he had with his son just before he left for college:

"I told him that I was proud of his passion, but that I wanted him to keep his options open. I suggested he might consider law school after college – that it could be a good foundation for any career, including journalism. Trey listened politely, but I could see in his eyes that his mind was made up. He was going to be a journalist, come what may."

The Move to Washington

In the fall of 2012, Trey packed his bags and headed to Washington, D.C., to begin his studies at American University. It was a significant move, not just geographically but symbolically. He was leaving behind the familiar surroundings of central Pennsylvania for the bustling, politically charged atmosphere of the capital.

Trey threw himself into his studies with characteristic enthusiasm. He declared a double major in Broadcast Journalism and International Relations, a combination that perfectly aligned with his career aspirations. His course load was demanding, but Trey thrived on the challenge.

From the beginning, Trey stood out among his peers. Professors noted his insatiable curiosity and his willingness to go above and beyond in his assignments. Dr. James Mitchell, who taught Trey in an introductory journalism course, remembers him as a student who was always pushing for more:

"Most freshmen are still finding their feet, but Trey arrived with a clear sense of purpose. He wasn't content with just completing assignments – he was always looking for ways to apply what he was learning to real-world situations. I remember him coming to my office hours to discuss how he could cover campus events in a more professional manner. His drive was impressive."

2. Entry into Journalism

First Steps in Reporting

Trey Yingst's entry into the world of professional journalism began long before he donned a press pass or stepped in front of a camera. His first true foray into reporting came during his sophomore year at American University, when he co-founded a news organization called News2Share with his classmate, Ford Fischer.

News2Share was born out of frustration. Trey and Ford felt that traditional media wasn't covering certain stories with the depth or perspective they deserved. They wanted to create a platform that would allow them to report on events as they saw them, without the constraints of established media narratives.

"We were young and maybe a bit naive," Trey recalled in a later interview. "But we believed we could make a difference by telling stories that weren't being told."

The fledgling news organization focused on on-the-ground reporting of protests, civil unrest, and political events. Trey and Ford would often be the only reporters at smaller demonstrations or town hall meetings, capturing moments that larger news outlets missed.

One of Trey's first significant stories for News2Share came in November 2014, when he covered the protests in Ferguson, Missouri, following the grand jury decision not to indict police officer Darren Wilson in the shooting of Michael Brown. Trey spent days on the streets of Ferguson, documenting the unrest and interviewing protesters and local residents. The experience was eye-opening for Trey. He found himself in the middle of a volatile situation, trying to maintain journalistic objectivity while witnessing intense emotions and occasional violence. His reports, shared through social media and picked up by some larger news outlets, provided a raw, unfiltered look at the events unfolding in Ferguson.

"I remember standing on a street corner, surrounded by tear gas, trying to keep my camera steady," Trey said. "That's when it really hit me – this is what I want to do with my life. This is how I can make a difference."

College Experiences and Internships

While News2Share was taking off, Trey continued to pursue other opportunities to hone his craft. He threw himself into his coursework at American University, excelling in classes on broadcast journalism, international relations, and media ethics. Professor Sarah Menke-Fish, who taught Trey in several advanced journalism courses, remembered him as a standout student. "Trey had a hunger for knowledge that set him apart," she said. "He wasn't just interested in the 'how' of journalism, but the 'why.' He wanted to understand the larger context of the stories he was covering."

Trey's academic performance opened doors for valuable internships. In the summer of 2015, he secured a position with a major network news organization in Washington, D.C. This internship gave him his first taste of a professional newsroom environment.

During his internship, Trey was assigned to the network's investigative unit. He spent hours poring over documents, fact-checking reports, and occasionally accompanying seasoned reporters on interviews. The experience taught him the importance of thorough research and the power of investigative journalism to effect change.

One of Trey's proudest moments during this internship came when he uncovered a lead that contributed to a major story about government waste. Though his role was small, seeing how his work fit into the larger investigative piece reinforced his belief in the importance of diligent, fact-based reporting.

Alongside his internship and coursework, Trey continued to push the boundaries with News2Share. He covered the 2016 presidential primaries, traveling to New Hampshire and South Carolina to report on campaign events and voter sentiments. This experience gave him valuable insights into political reporting and the challenges of covering a national campaign.

Breaking into Broadcast

As Trey approached graduation, he began to set his sights on the next step in his career. His goal was to become a on-air reporter, preferably covering international news and conflicts. However, he knew that breaking into broadcast journalism, especially at a national level, would be challenging.

Trey's break came through a connection he had made during his time with News2Share. An executive at One America News Network (OANN) had been impressed by Trey's on-the-ground reporting and offered him a position as a field reporter in Washington, D.C.

The job at OANN was a significant step for Trey. Though the network was smaller and less established than the major cable news channels, it offered him the opportunity to report on national politics and occasionally on international events.

Trey threw himself into his new role with characteristic enthusiasm. He was often the first reporter in the office and the last to leave, constantly pitching story ideas and volunteering for challenging assignments. His dedication paid off. Within months, Trey had become one of OANN's most visible reporters, covering everything from Congressional hearings to international summits. His reports were noted for their clarity and his ability to break down complex political issues for viewers.

The White House Beat

Trey's big break at OANN came when he was assigned to cover the White House. At just 23 years old, he became one of the youngest correspondents to hold a hard pass for the White House press corps.

The White House beat was intense and competitive. Trey found himself surrounded by veteran journalists from major news organizations, all vying for the same stories and sound bites. But rather than being intimidated, Trey saw this as an opportunity to learn and to prove himself. He quickly gained a reputation for asking tough, incisive questions during press briefings. His colleagues noted his thorough preparation and his willingness to follow up when he felt an answer was incomplete or evasive.

One memorable moment came during a briefing with then-Press Secretary Sarah Huckabee Sanders. Trey pressed for details on the administration's Syria policy, refusing to accept vague answers. His persistent questioning led to a tense exchange that made headlines and earned him respect from fellow reporters.

"Trey wasn't afraid to ruffle feathers," said veteran White House correspondent Jim Acosta. "He came in with the attitude that he had just as much right to be there as anyone else, and he wasn't going to waste the opportunity."

International Aspirations

While Trey was making a name for himself on the White House beat, his ambitions remained focused on international reporting. He used every opportunity to pitch stories with a global focus, and eagerly took on assignments that required travel.

In 2017, Trey got his first taste of reporting from a conflict zone when he was sent to cover tensions along the Israel-Gaza border. The assignment was challenging and potentially dangerous, but Trey embraced it with enthusiasm.

His reports from Israel and Gaza showcased his ability to provide clear, concise explanations of complex geopolitical situations. He also demonstrated a knack for finding human interest stories that helped viewers connect with the larger political narrative. This assignment confirmed for Trey that his true calling lay in international reporting. He returned to Washington more determined than ever to find a position that would allow him to cover global events full-time.

The Move to Fox News

Trey's work at OANN had not gone unnoticed by larger networks. In 2018, he was approached by Fox News with an offer to join their team as a general assignment reporter based in Jerusalem.

The decision to leave OANN was not an easy one. The network had given Trey his first big break, and he had built strong relationships with his colleagues. However, the opportunity to report from the Middle East for a major network was too good to pass up.

"I knew this was the chance I had been waiting for," Trey said. "It was a big step, and honestly, it was a bit scary. But I also knew that if I wanted to become the kind of journalist I aspired to be, I had to take risks."

In September 2018, at the age of 25, Trey moved to Jerusalem to begin his new role with Fox News. The position would place him at the center of one of the world's most volatile regions, covering stories that had global implications.

Learning the Ropes in a New Environment

Trey's first few months in Jerusalem were a whirlwind of activity. He had to quickly familiarize himself with the intricacies of Middle Eastern politics, build a network of sources, and adapt to the challenges of reporting from a region where tensions could flare at any moment.

He threw himself into the work, spending long hours in the field and devoting his free time to studying the history and culture of the region. Trey was determined to provide reporting that went beyond surface-level analysis and offered viewers genuine insights into the stories he was covering.

One of Trey's early assignments for Fox News was to report on the ongoing Syrian Civil War. He traveled to the Syrian-Israeli border in the Golan Heights, where he produced a series of reports on the impact of the conflict on local communities and the broader geopolitical implications.

These reports showcased Trey's ability to break down complex situations for viewers back home. He combined on-the-ground reporting with clear explanations of the historical and political context, earning praise from both viewers and his colleagues at Fox.

Building a Reputation

As Trey settled into his role, he began to make a name for himself as a reliable and insightful correspondent. His reports were noted for their balance and depth, and he quickly became a regular presence on Fox News' primetime shows.

Trey's colleagues at Fox were impressed by his work ethic and his willingness to go the extra mile for a story. Greg Palkot, a veteran foreign correspondent for Fox News, noted, "Trey has a rare combination of talents. He's got the nose of a seasoned reporter, the energy of a newcomer, and the ability to explain complex situations in a way that viewers can understand. That's a powerful combination in this business."

One of Trey's most significant early assignments came in March 2019, when he was sent to cover the final battle against ISIS in Syria. Reporting from the frontlines, Trey provided viewers with a first-hand look at the fall of the last ISIS stronghold in Baghouz.

This assignment was not without risks. Trey found himself in dangerous situations, including being caught in the crossfire during one particularly intense day of fighting. However, his reports from

Syria further cemented his reputation as a correspondent willing to go where the story was, no matter the personal risk.

3. Rise to Prominence

Notable Assignments Pre-2023

As Trey Yingst entered the 2020s, his career trajectory continued its steep upward climb. The young reporter who had cut his teeth on the streets of Ferguson and in the White House press room was about to face some of the most challenging and defining moments of his career.

The COVID-19 Pandemic

The outbreak of the COVID-19 pandemic in early 2020 presented unprecedented challenges for journalists worldwide. For Trey, based in Jerusalem, it meant adapting to new ways of reporting while covering the impact of the virus in a region already fraught with tension.

In March 2020, as Israel implemented strict lockdown measures, Trey found himself reporting from eerily empty streets in Jerusalem's Old City. His reports captured the surreal atmosphere of holy sites devoid of pilgrims and tourists, providing viewers with a stark visual representation of the pandemic's global reach.

But Trey's coverage went beyond mere observation. He delved into the political and social implications of the pandemic in the region, reporting on how the virus was affecting Israeli-Palestinian relations and exacerbating existing inequalities.

One of Trey's most impactful stories during this period focused on the challenges faced by Gaza's healthcare system in dealing with the pandemic. His report, which involved remote interviews with doctors in Gaza and analysis of data from international health organizations, shed light on a critical situation that was receiving little attention in Western media.

The Abraham Accords

As the world grappled with the pandemic, a significant geopolitical shift was taking place in the Middle East. The Abraham Accords, a series of agreements normalizing relations between Israel and several Arab states, represented a historic change in regional dynamics.

Trey was at the forefront of covering these developments. He reported live from the White House lawn during the signing ceremony in September 2020, providing viewers with context and analysis of the agreements' significance.

In the months that followed, Trey traveled extensively throughout the region, reporting on the practical implications of the Accords. He was one of the first Western journalists to report from the

United Arab Emirates following the normalization of relations with Israel, offering viewers a glimpse into the rapidly changing social and economic landscape.

One of Trey's most memorable reports from this period came from a synagogue in Dubai, where he interviewed members of the city's small but growing Jewish community. His report humanized the geopolitical shift, showing how the Accords were impacting ordinary people's lives.

The Israel-Gaza Conflict of 2021

In May 2021, Trey found himself covering one of the most intense periods of conflict between Israel and Hamas in recent years. Over 11 days, he reported from various locations in Israel and along the Gaza border, often broadcasting live as rockets flew overhead. Trey's coverage during this period was noted for its balance and depth. He reported on the impact of Hamas rockets on Israeli communities while also covering the devastating effects of Israeli airstrikes on Gaza. His ability to provide clear, factual reporting in the midst of a highly charged and emotional conflict earned him praise from colleagues and viewers alike.

One particularly harrowing moment came when Trey was reporting live from Ashkelon, a city in southern Israel. As he was speaking on camera, the sound of incoming rocket sirens forced him and his crew to take cover. The incident, which was broadcast live, highlighted the dangers faced by journalists in conflict zones and added a visceral reality to Trey's reporting.

Development of Reporting Style

Throughout these assignments, Trey continued to refine and develop his reporting style. His approach was characterized by several key elements that set him apart from many of his peers.

On-the-Ground Presence

Trey firmly believed in the importance of being physically present where news was happening. He often said, "You can't truly understand a story unless you're there, seeing it with your own eyes, smelling the air, feeling the tension or excitement."

This commitment to on-the-ground reporting sometimes put Trey in dangerous situations, but it also allowed him to provide viewers with a level of detail and authenticity that was hard to match. Whether he was dodging rockets in Ashkelon or navigating the complex social dynamics of the UAE post-Abraham Accords, Trey's reports always carried the weight of first-hand experience.

Contextual Reporting

One of Trey's strengths was his ability to provide context to the events he was covering. He understood that many viewers might not be familiar with the historical and cultural background of the stories he was reporting on, especially in the complex landscape of the Middle East.

To address this, Trey developed a style of reporting that seamlessly wove background information into his coverage of current events. He became adept at explaining complex geopolitical situations in clear, concise terms without oversimplifying or losing nuance.

This approach was evident in his coverage of the Abraham Accords. Rather than simply reporting on the signing ceremony, Trey provided viewers with a comprehensive understanding of the historical significance of the agreements, the motivations of the various parties involved, and the potential long-term implications for the region.

Human-Centric Storytelling

While Trey excelled at covering major geopolitical events, he never lost sight of the human element in his stories. He made a point of seeking out and amplifying the voices of ordinary people affected by the events he was covering.

During the 2021 Israel-Gaza conflict, for example, Trey's reports often included interviews with civilians on both sides of the border. He spoke with Israeli families living under the threat of rocket attacks and with Palestinian families in Gaza dealing with the aftermath of airstrikes. These personal stories helped viewers connect with the human cost of the conflict in a way that statistics and political analysis alone could not.

Technological Integration

As a young journalist who had grown up in the digital age, Trey was quick to embrace new technologies in his reporting. He was an early adopter of social media as a tool for newsgathering and dissemination, often using Twitter to share real-time updates from the field.

Trey also experimented with new forms of visual storytelling. He began incorporating drone footage into his reports, providing viewers with unique perspectives on the stories he was covering. During his coverage of the Abraham Accords, for example, he used drone shots to showcase the rapid development taking place in the UAE, visually representing the economic opportunities that normalization with Israel was expected to bring.

Establishment as a Respected War Correspondent

By 2022, Trey Yingst had firmly established himself as one of the most respected young war correspondents in the field. His coverage of conflicts and major geopolitical events had earned him recognition from both viewers and fellow journalists.

Industry Recognition

Trey's work began to receive formal recognition from the journalism industry. In 2022, he was awarded the prestigious Overseas Press Club Award for his coverage of the 2021 Israel-Gaza conflict. The judges praised his "courage under fire and commitment to presenting a balanced picture of a complex and emotionally charged situation."

This award was a significant milestone in Trey's career. At 29, he was one of the youngest journalists to receive this honor, placing him in the company of some of the most renowned names in international journalism.

Peer Respect

Perhaps even more meaningful than formal awards was the respect Trey had earned from his peers in the field. Veteran war correspondents praised his work ethic, his courage, and his commitment to ethical journalism.

Christiane Amanpour, one of Trey's childhood idols, commented on his work during a panel discussion on war reporting: "What impresses me about Trey Yingst is not just his bravery, which is evident, but his dedication to getting the story right. In an age of instant news and social media, he takes the time to understand and explain the context of the stories he's covering. That's increasingly rare and incredibly valuable."

Expanded Responsibilities

As Trey's reputation grew, so did his responsibilities at Fox News. By late 2022, he was no longer just a foreign correspondent based in Jerusalem, but had become the network's go-to reporter for major international stories across the Middle East and beyond.

This expanded role saw Trey traveling more frequently, covering stories from the ongoing civil war in Syria to political upheavals in Lebanon and Iraq. He also began to appear more regularly on the network's opinion shows, where his firsthand experience and understanding of Middle Eastern politics made him a valuable contributor to broader discussions on U.S. foreign policy.

Mentorship and Inspiration

As Trey's profile rose, he also began to take on a mentorship role for younger journalists. He frequently spoke at journalism schools and industry conferences, sharing his experiences and offering advice to those looking to follow in his footsteps.

In these talks, Trey often emphasized the importance of preparation, perseverance, and ethical reporting. "This job isn't about adrenaline or being on TV," he would say. "It's about bearing witness to history and helping people understand the world around them. That's a huge responsibility, and it's one we have to take seriously every single day."

Trey's success and his willingness to share his knowledge inspired a new generation of journalists. Many young reporters cited him as a role model, admiring not just his on-camera presence but his dedication to the craft of journalism.

Looking Ahead

As 2023 dawned, Trey Yingst stood at the pinnacle of his career thus far. At just 30 years old, he had already achieved more than many journalists do in a lifetime. He had covered wars, interviewed world leaders, and brought critical stories to global attention.

But for Trey, this was just the beginning. He remained as hungry for the next big story as he had been as a college student starting News2Share. He continued to push himself, always looking for new ways to improve his reporting and to bring important stories to light.

Little did Trey know that the biggest test of his career was just months away. The events of October 7th, 2023, would challenge him like nothing before, pushing his skills, his courage, and his commitment to journalism to their very limits. But the experiences he had gained, the skills he had honed, and the reputation he had built over the past decade had prepared him for this moment. When the call came, Trey Yingst was ready to tell the story that would define not just his career, but an entire era in Middle Eastern history.

Part II: The Lead-up to October 7th

4. Geopolitical Context

To understand the events of October 7th, 2023, we must first examine the historical and political landscape that set the stage for that fateful day. The Israel-Palestine conflict, with its deep roots and far-reaching consequences, forms the backdrop against which this tragedy unfolded.

Brief History of the Israel-Palestine Conflict

The origins of the Israel-Palestine conflict trace back to the late 19th and early 20th centuries. As the Zionist movement gained momentum among Jewish communities worldwide, advocating for a Jewish homeland in the historical region of Palestine, tensions began to rise with the local Arab population. The end of World War I saw the collapse of the Ottoman Empire, which had ruled the region for centuries. The British Mandate for Palestine, established in 1920, set the stage for increasing Jewish immigration and growing Arab resistance. The conflicting promises made by the British to both Jewish and Arab leaders during this period sowed the seeds of future conflict.

The Birth of Israel and the First Arab-Israeli War

In 1947, the United Nations proposed a partition plan for Palestine, dividing the territory into separate Jewish and Arab states. While Jewish leaders accepted the plan, Arab leaders rejected it, leading to a civil war. On May 14, 1948, David Ben-Gurion proclaimed the establishment of the State of Israel, triggering the first Arab-Israeli War.

The war ended in 1949 with Israel's victory and the expansion of its territory beyond the UN partition plan boundaries. This conflict resulted in the displacement of hundreds of thousands of Palestinians, an event known as the Nakba (catastrophe) in Palestinian narratives.

Subsequent Wars and Peace Attempts

The decades following Israel's establishment saw several more wars, including the Six-Day War of 1967, which resulted in Israel occupying the West Bank, East Jerusalem, Gaza Strip, Sinai Peninsula, and Golan Heights. The 1973 Yom Kippur War and the 1982 Lebanon War further shaped the region's geopolitical landscape.

Attempts at peace began in earnest with the 1978 Camp David Accords between Israel and Egypt, leading to a peace treaty in 1979. The Oslo Accords of the 1990s brought hope for a two-state solution, but ultimately failed to resolve core issues such as borders, Jerusalem's status, and the right of return for Palestinian refugees.

The Second Intifada and Beyond

The collapse of the Camp David Summit in 2000 led to the Second Intifada, a period of intensified Israeli-Palestinian violence. This era saw the rise of suicide bombings by Palestinian militants and increased military operations by Israel in the West Bank and Gaza.

In 2005, Israel unilaterally withdrew from the Gaza Strip, dismantling all Israeli settlements in the area. However, this did not end the conflict. Hamas, an Islamist militant group, took control of Gaza in 2007, leading to a de facto division of Palestinian governance between the Hamas-controlled Gaza Strip and the Fatah-led Palestinian Authority in the West Bank.

Recent Developments and Tensions

The years leading up to 2023 saw a series of events that further complicated the Israeli-Palestinian conflict and set the stage for the October 7th attacks.

The Trump Era and the Abraham Accords

The presidency of Donald Trump marked a significant shift in U.S. policy towards the conflict. In 2017, Trump recognized Jerusalem as Israel's capital and moved the U.S. Embassy there, a decision that sparked widespread protests among Palestinians and criticism from much of the international community.

In 2020, the Trump administration brokered the Abraham Accords, normalizing relations between Israel and several Arab states, including the United Arab Emirates, Bahrain, Sudan, and Morocco.

While hailed as a diplomatic breakthrough by some, these agreements were seen by Palestinians as a betrayal of their cause.

Gaza Conflicts and Escalating Tensions

The period between 2008 and 2023 saw several rounds of intense fighting between Israel and Hamas in Gaza. Operations like "Cast Lead" (2008-2009), "Pillar of Defense" (2012), "Protective Edge" (2014), and the conflict in May 2021 resulted in significant casualties on both sides and widespread destruction in Gaza.

These conflicts were characterized by Hamas rocket attacks on Israeli civilians and Israeli airstrikes on Gaza, with each side accusing the other of war crimes. The international community repeatedly called for ceasefires and a return to negotiations, but a lasting solution remained elusive.

Internal Political Challenges

Both Israeli and Palestinian politics underwent significant upheavals in the years preceding 2023. In Israel, a series of inconclusive elections led to political instability, with Benjamin Netanyahu's long tenure as Prime Minister ending in 2021, only for him to return to power in late 2022 at the head of a coalition that included far-right parties.

On the Palestinian side, the divide between Hamas in Gaza and the Palestinian Authority in the West Bank deepened. Attempts at reconciliation and plans for elections repeatedly faltered, leaving the Palestinian people without a unified leadership.

Settlements and Annexation Debates

The expansion of Israeli settlements in the West Bank remained a major point of contention. Despite international criticism, settlement construction continued, with some Israeli politicians advocating for the formal annexation of parts of the West Bank. These moves were seen by Palestinians and much of the international community as undermining the viability of a future Palestinian state.

The State of Affairs in Early October 2023

As October 2023 dawned, the situation in Israel and the Palestinian territories was a powder keg waiting to explode. Several factors contributed to the heightened tensions that would ultimately lead to the events of October 7th.

Political Instability in Israel

Israel's government, led once again by Benjamin Netanyahu, was facing significant domestic challenges. Protests against judicial reforms proposed by the government had been ongoing for months, creating deep divisions within Israeli society. This internal strife had raised concerns about the country's readiness to face external threats.

Economic Pressures in Gaza

The Gaza Strip, under Hamas control and subject to a blockade by Israel and Egypt, was facing severe economic hardship. Unemployment rates were sky-high, particularly among young people, and basic services like electricity and clean water were in short supply. This desperation created fertile ground for extremist ideologies and actions.

Religious Tensions in Jerusalem

The status of Jerusalem, particularly the Old City and its holy sites, remained a flashpoint. Incidents at the Al-Aqsa Mosque compound, revered by both Muslims and Jews (who know it as the Temple Mount), had the potential to spark wider conflicts. In the weeks leading up to October 7th, there had been several clashes between Israeli security forces and Palestinian worshippers at the site.

Regional Dynamics

The broader Middle East was in a state of flux. The Abraham Accords had altered traditional alliances, with some Arab states moving closer to Israel. However, Iran's influence in the region, particularly its support for groups like Hamas and Hezbollah, remained a significant concern for Israel and its allies.

International Attention Elsewhere

Global attention in early October 2023 was largely focused on other international crises, including the ongoing war in Ukraine and tensions between China and Taiwan. This relative lack of international focus on the Israeli-Palestinian conflict may have contributed to a sense that the time was ripe for dramatic action.

Security Complacency

Despite the tensions, there was a degree of complacency on the Israeli side regarding the threat from Gaza. The Iron Dome missile defense system had proved highly effective in previous conflicts, and there was a belief that Hamas's capabilities had been significantly degraded in previous rounds of fighting. This sense of security would prove tragically misplaced on October 7th.

Hamas's Internal Dynamics

Within Hamas, there were internal debates about strategy and tactics. Some factions were pushing for a more aggressive approach, arguing that only dramatic action could change the status quo. The decision to launch the October 7th attacks would have been the result of intense discussions and planning within the organization's leadership. As the first week of October 2023 unfolded, few could have predicted the scale and brutality of what was to come. The long-standing conflict, with its deep historical roots and recent exacerbating factors, was about to enter a new and terrible phase.

Trey Yingst, who had spent years covering the region and its conflicts, was well aware of these underlying tensions. His deep understanding of the historical context and current dynamics would prove invaluable as he reported on the events that were about to unfold. However, even with his experience and knowledge, nothing could have fully prepared him for what he would witness on October 7th and in the days that followed.

The stage was set, the actors were in place, and the world was about to be shocked by a day that would redefine the Israeli-Palestinian conflict and test the limits of human endurance and journalistic courage.

5. Trey Yingst in Israel

Assignment Details

In the early days of October 2023, Trey Yingst found himself back in familiar territory. His assignment in Israel was not unusual; he had been covering the region for Fox News for several years. However, this time, there was a different feeling in the air, a tension that even the experienced correspondent couldn't quite put his finger on.

Trey's official brief from Fox News was broad: cover the ongoing developments in Israel and the Palestinian territories, with a focus on the increasing tensions in Jerusalem and the Gaza border. The network valued Trey's ability to provide context and details to complex situations, and they trusted him to find the stories that would resonate with their viewers.

"We need you to be our eyes and ears on the ground," his producer had told him during their last call before he left for Israel. "There's a lot of chatter about potential escalations, but nothing concrete. Keep your ear to the ground and be ready for anything."

This open-ended assignment was both a challenge and an opportunity for Trey. It allowed him the freedom to pursue the stories he found most compelling, but it also meant he had to be constantly alert, ready to pivot at a moment's notice if events took an unexpected turn.

The Team

Trey wasn't working alone. He was accompanied by his trusted cameraman, Jake, with whom he had worked on numerous assignments over the years.

Jake's steady hand and keen eye complemented Trey's reporting style perfectly. They had developed an almost telepathic understanding over time, with Jake often anticipating Trey's movements during live shots or in tense situations.

The team also included a local producer, Mira, whose knowledge of Hebrew and Arabic, as well as her extensive network of contacts, was invaluable. Mira had worked with various international news organizations over the years, and her insights often provided Trey with leads that other reporters missed.

Base of Operations

Fox News had set up Trey and his team in a small apartment in Jerusalem. The location was strategic, allowing quick access to both the Old City, where tensions often flared, and major roads leading to other parts of Israel and the West Bank. The apartment was spartan but functional. Maps of Israel and the Palestinian territories covered one wall, marked with potential hotspots and the locations of recent incidents. A bank of monitors allowed the team to keep track of local news channels and social media feeds, essential tools for staying ahead of breaking news.

Preparation and Expectations

Trey's preparation for this assignment began long before he set foot in Israel. His years of experience covering the region had given him a deep well of knowledge to draw from, but he knew that in this fast-changing environment, he needed to be as up-to-date as possible.

Research and Briefings

In the weeks leading up to his departure, Trey immersed himself in the latest reports and analyses on the situation in Israel and the Palestinian territories. He pored over academic papers, think tank reports, and journalistic accounts, building a comprehensive picture of the current state of affairs. He also arranged briefings with experts in the field. A Skype call with a professor of Middle Eastern studies at Georgetown University provided valuable historical context. An off-the-record conversation with a State Department official gave him insights into the U.S. government's current stance on the Israeli-Palestinian conflict.

Trey's notebook filled up with names, dates, and potential story ideas. He was particularly interested in exploring the impact of the Abraham Accords on Palestinian public opinion and the growing dissatisfaction with both the Palestinian Authority and Hamas leadership.

Equipment Check

The technical aspects of the job were just as important as the intellectual preparation. Trey and

Jake spent a full day going through their equipment, ensuring everything was in working order. They packed extra batteries, memory cards, and even a satellite phone for emergencies.

Trey paid special attention to his protective gear. He had learned the hard way about the importance of a good flak jacket and helmet. "Better to have it and not need it, than need it and not have it," he often said. Little did he know how crucial this equipment would prove to be in the days to come.

Mental Preparation

Perhaps the most challenging aspect of preparation was mental. Trey had covered conflicts before, but each assignment brought its own set of psychological challenges. He knew the importance of maintaining objectivity while also staying empathetic to the human stories he would encounter.

In the quiet moments before sleep, Trey often found himself thinking about the potential scenarios he might face. He visualized himself reporting under pressure, asking tough questions, and maintaining his composure in dangerous situations. This mental rehearsal was a crucial part of his preparation process.

Expectations

As for what to expect on this assignment, Trey tried to keep an open mind. His experience had taught him that situations in this region could change rapidly and unpredictably. However, based on his research and briefings, he had some general expectations:

1. Increased tensions around Jerusalem's holy sites, particularly the Al-Aqsa Mosque compound.

2. Potential for demonstrations or clashes in the West Bank, especially near Israeli settlements.
3. Possible escalation of rocket fire from Gaza and retaliatory strikes by Israel.
4. Ongoing political uncertainty in Israel and its potential impact on relations with the Palestinians.

Trey shared these expectations with his team, but also emphasized the need for flexibility. "We need to be ready for anything," he told Jake and Mira during their first team meeting in Jerusalem. "Our job is to be where the story is, wherever that might take us."

The Calm Before the Storm

The first few days of October passed in a rhythm familiar to seasoned journalists in conflict zones - a mix of intense activity and periods of waiting. Trey and his team crisscrossed Jerusalem and its surroundings, gathering background material and conducting interviews for potential feature stories.

On the Streets of Jerusalem

One crisp morning, Trey found himself walking through the narrow alleys of Jerusalem's Old City. The ancient stones seemed to whisper stories of centuries of conflict and coexistence. He stopped to buy a cup of strong, sweet coffee from a Palestinian vendor, engaging in a brief conversation about the recent tensions at the Al-Aqsa Mosque.

"Things are not good," the vendor said, shaking his head. "Everyone is angry. Everyone is afraid. Who knows what will happen next?"

Trey nodded, jotting down notes. These street-level conversations often provided more insight than official statements. He made a mental note to include this perspective in his next report.

At the Gaza Border

A day trip to the Gaza border provided a stark contrast to the bustling streets of Jerusalem. Trey stood on a hilltop, gazing out at the Gaza Strip in the distance. The landscape was eerily quiet, but the tension was palpable.

An Israeli Defense Forces (IDF) spokesperson gave Trey a briefing on the recent security measures implemented along the border. The officer spoke of advanced surveillance systems and underground barriers designed to prevent infiltration.

"We're always prepared," the officer said confidently. "Hamas knows they can't surprise us."

Trey nodded, but something about the officer's certainty made him uneasy. He had learned over the years that in this region, certainty was often misplaced.

Conversations with Locals

In the evenings, Trey would often sit in cafes or restaurants, striking up conversations with locals. He spoke with Israeli students worried about the political situation, Palestinian workers frustrated with the economic conditions, and foreign tourists trying to make sense of it all.

One conversation stood out. An elderly Israeli man, a veteran of several wars, shared his perspective:

"I've seen so much conflict in my life," he said, his eyes distant. "But something feels different now. There's a tension in the air. It reminds me of the calm before the Yom Kippur War."

Trey listened intently, recording the man's words. He couldn't shake the feeling that this old soldier might be onto something.

The Night Before

On the evening of October 6th, Trey sat on the balcony of his apartment, looking out over the Jerusalem skyline. The city seemed peaceful, the golden light of sunset bathing the ancient stones in a warm glow. It was hard to imagine that this serene scene could be the backdrop for the conflict he had come to cover.

He reviewed his notes from the past few days, trying to piece together a coherent narrative from the various interviews and observations. There were signs of increasing tensions, certainly, but nothing that pointed to an imminent crisis.

Mira joined him on the balcony, bringing a fresh round of coffee. "Any plans for tomorrow?" she asked.

Trey shook his head. "It's Shabbat, so things should be quiet. I thought we might head to the Old City, maybe get some atmosphere shots for a feature on the current mood in Jerusalem."

Mira nodded, but there was a hint of concern in her eyes. "I've been hearing some chatter on social media," she said. "Nothing specific, but there's a lot of angry talk. More than usual."

Trey made a note to check the online chatter in the morning. In this region, social media could often be a barometer for upcoming events.

As night fell, Trey prepared for bed, setting his alarm for an early start. He had no way of knowing that in just a few hours, he would be woken not by his alarm, but by the sound of explosions. The storm that had been brewing was about to break, and Trey Yingst would find himself at the center of one of the most shocking and violent days in recent Middle Eastern history. The calm of that October night was deceptive. In the Gaza Strip, final preparations were being made for an attack that would shake Israel to its core. In Israeli towns and kibbutzim near the Gaza border, families were settling in for what they expected to be a peaceful Shabbat.

And in his Jerusalem apartment, Trey Yingst slept, unaware that he was about to face the biggest challenge of his career - reporting on a day that would forever be etched in the annals of the Israeli-Palestinian conflict.

The stage was set. The actors were in place. And as the first light of dawn approached on October 7th, 2023, the world held its breath, unaware of the horror that was about to unfold.

Part III: October 7th, 2023 - The Day Unfolds

6. Dawn Breaks: The Initial Attacks

The first light of October 7th, 2023, crept over the horizon, painting the sky in soft hues of pink and gold. It was a Sabbath morning in Israel, traditionally a day of rest and peace. But on this day, the tranquility would be shattered in ways no one could have foreseen.

First Reports and Confusion

At 6:30 AM local time, the silence of the early morning was abruptly broken by the wail of air raid sirens. In communities near the Gaza Strip, residents were jolted awake, many scrambling for shelter with practiced urgency. For them, rocket alerts were an unwelcome but not unfamiliar occurrence. However, what followed was far from routine.

The Initial Barrage

Within minutes, the skies over southern and central Israel were filled with a massive barrage of rockets. The sheer scale of the attack was unprecedented. Estimates would later put the number of rockets fired in the initial volley at over 2,000, overwhelming Israel's Iron Dome defense system.

The first reports began to trickle in through various channels. Local news stations interrupted their regular programming with urgent alerts. Social media platforms exploded with posts from frightened residents, many sharing videos of rockets streaking across the sky or the sound of explosions in the distance.

Confusion Reigns

In the first hour, confusion reigned. The Israeli military, caught off guard by the scale and coordination of the attack, struggled to assess the situation and respond. Initial statements were vague, urging residents in the south to stay in shelters but providing little additional information.

As dawn fully broke, reports began to emerge of something even more alarming than the rocket attacks. There were unconfirmed accounts of armed militants crossing the border from Gaza into Israeli territory. These reports, at first dismissed by many as rumors or exaggerations, would soon prove to be horrifyingly true.

Breaking News Alerts

News organizations around the world began to pick up on the unfolding events. Breaking news alerts flashed across screens, initially reporting a "significant escalation" in hostilities between Israel and Hamas. But the true nature and scale of what was happening had yet to become clear.

In newsrooms across Israel and internationally, journalists scrambled to verify information and make sense of the rapidly evolving situation. The challenge was immense – separating fact from rumor in a chaotic environment where even official sources seemed unsure of what was happening.

Trey's Location and Initial Reactions

As the first rockets were launched from Gaza, Trey Yingst was asleep in his apartment in Jerusalem, about 50 miles from the Gaza border. The distant sound of explosions, rather than his alarm clock, jolted him awake.

A Rude Awakening

Trey's years of experience in conflict zones had honed his instincts. Even before he was fully awake, he knew something significant was happening. He jumped out of bed, quickly dressed, and moved to the apartment's small operations room where monitors displayed various news channels.

The scenes unfolding on the screens confirmed his suspicions – this was no ordinary rocket attack. Trey immediately reached for his phone, dialing his producer back in New York.

"Something big is happening," he said, his voice tense but controlled. "We need to go live as soon as possible."

Assessing the Situation

As Trey waited for his team to assemble, he began the process of trying to understand what was happening. He flipped between news channels, scrolled through social media feeds, and made rapid-fire calls to his network of sources. The picture that emerged was fragmented and alarming. Rockets were falling across a wide swath of Israel. There were unconfirmed reports of gunfire in Israeli communities near the Gaza border. The Israeli military seemed to be caught flat-footed, its responses confused and contradictory.

Trey's mind raced as he tried to piece together the information. His years of covering the region told him that this was unlike anything he had seen before. The scale, the coordination, the apparent breach of the border – all pointed to something unprecedented.

Team Assembly

Within thirty minutes of the first sirens, Trey's team had assembled in the apartment. His cameraman,

Jake, arrived first, already setting up equipment for a potential live shot. Mira, their local producer, rushed in soon after, her phone glued to her ear as she spoke rapidly in Hebrew to a contact.

The team huddled around the monitors, sharing what information they had gathered. Mira's local contacts were proving invaluable, providing details that hadn't yet made it to the mainstream media.

"I'm hearing reports of gunmen in Sderot," Mira said, her voice tight with tension. "And there's chaos at the police dispatch center. They're overwhelmed with calls."

Decision Time

Trey faced a crucial decision. As a journalist, his instinct was to get as close to the story as possible. The most intense fighting seemed to be happening near the Gaza border. But the situation was chaotic and potentially extremely dangerous.

"We need to get down there," Trey said, his eyes fixed on a map of southern Israel. "But we need to be smart about this. Jake, check our protective gear. Mira, see if you can find us a reliable driver who knows the area."

As his team sprang into action, Trey took a moment to center himself. He closed his eyes, took a deep breath, and mentally prepared for what he knew would be one of the most challenging days of his career.

The First Broadcast

At 7:45 AM, just over an hour after the initial attacks began, Trey went live on Fox News. Standing on the balcony of his Jerusalem apartment, with the Old City visible in the background, he delivered his first report of the day.

"Good morning. I'm Trey Yingst in Jerusalem. Israel is under attack. A massive barrage of rockets has been launched from Gaza, targeting cities and towns across the country. But this is more than just a rocket attack. We're receiving reports of armed militants crossing into Israeli territory. The situation is fluid and dangerous."

As he spoke, the sound of distant explosions could be heard. Trey's voice was steady, but the gravity of the situation was evident in his expression.

"The Israeli military appears to have been caught by surprise. Their response so far has been limited and confused. This is a developing situation, and we'll bring you updates as we get them."

As the camera cut away, Trey immediately turned to his team. "We need to move. Now."

On the Road

By 8:30 AM, Trey and his team were in a car, heading south towards the Gaza border. The highways were eerily empty, save for military vehicles racing in the opposite direction. Occasionally, they could see streaks of rocket fire in the sky, followed by the bright flashes of Iron Dome interceptors.

As they drove, Trey was on the phone constantly – speaking with sources, coordinating with his producers in New York, and trying to gather more information about what was happening.

The car radio was tuned to an Israeli news station. The reports coming in were growing increasingly dire. There were accounts of gunmen in multiple Israeli communities. The death toll, still unconfirmed, was rising rapidly.

Trey felt a knot in his stomach. In all his years of covering conflicts, he had never experienced anything quite like this. The scale of the attack, the apparent breach of Israeli defenses – it was all unprecedented. As they approached the city of Ashkelon, about 8 miles north of the Gaza Strip, the reality of the situation became even more apparent. They could hear the steady thump of artillery fire and the whoosh of rockets overhead. Smoke rose from several locations on the horizon.

Trey turned to Jake, his voice somber. "Whatever we thought we were driving into, I think the reality is going to be much worse."

Jake nodded grimly, checking his camera equipment one more time.

In that moment, as they drove towards the epicenter of the unfolding catastrophe, Trey Yingst steeled himself for what lay ahead. He knew that the events of this day would likely define his career as a journalist. More importantly, he understood the weight of the responsibility he carried – to bear witness to history, to tell the stories of those caught in this maelstrom, and to help the world understand the magnitude of what was unfolding.

The sun was now fully up, casting a harsh light over the Israeli landscape. But for Trey Yingst and countless others, the true darkness of October 7th, 2023, was just beginning to reveal itself.

7. Morning: Chaos Spreads

Key Incidents and Locations

As the morning of October 7th progressed, the true scale and horror of the attacks began to emerge. What had initially seemed like an unusually large rocket barrage was revealed to be a coordinated, multi-pronged assault on Israeli territory. The chaos that had begun at dawn spread rapidly, engulfing multiple locations and leaving Israeli security forces scrambling to respond.

Breach of the Gaza Border Fence

One of the most shocking aspects of the attack was the breach of the heavily fortified Gaza border fence. Hamas militants, using a combination of explosives and heavy machinery, had created multiple gaps in the barrier that Israel had long relied on for protection. Through these breaches, hundreds of armed militants poured into Israeli territory.

The Israeli military, caught off guard by the audacity and scale of the incursion, struggled to mount an effective response in the early hours. The defensive systems and protocols that had been developed over years proved inadequate in the face of this unprecedented assault.

Attacks on Civilian Communities

Some of the most horrific incidents of the day occurred in the Israeli communities near the Gaza border. Towns and kibbutzim that had long lived under the threat of rocket fire now faced a far more immediate and terrifying danger.

In Sderot, a town that had often been targeted by rockets from Gaza, residents awoke to the sound of gunfire in their streets. Hamas militants moved through the town, attacking homes and public buildings. The local police station, a symbol of security for the community, was one of the first targets, leaving the town's residents even more vulnerable.

Further south, the kibbutzim of Nahal Oz and Be'eri became scenes of unimaginable horror. Militants breached these small, tight-knit communities, going house to house. Reports began to emerge of civilians being killed in their homes, of families being taken hostage, of people desperately trying to hide or flee.

The Nova Music Festival Massacre

Perhaps one of the most shocking incidents of the morning occurred at the Nova music festival, an all-night rave being held in a rural area near Kibbutz Re'im. As dawn broke and the festival was winding down, the thousands of young people in attendance suddenly found themselves under attack.

Hamas militants, who had infiltrated the area, opened fire on the crowd. The scene quickly devolved into chaos, with festival-goers desperately trying to escape. Many were gunned down as they ran. Others were taken hostage. The open fields that had been a place of celebration just hours before became a killing ground.

Military Bases Targeted

It wasn't just civilian targets that came under attack. Several Israeli military bases near the Gaza border were also hit. The Zikim base, home to the IDF's Gaza Division, was one of the first to be attacked. The militants' ability to penetrate these heavily guarded facilities added to the sense of shock and disbelief that was spreading through Israeli society.

Escalation in the North

As if the situation in the south wasn't dire enough, reports began to come in of rocket fire from Lebanon towards northern Israel. Hezbollah, the Lebanese militant group and longtime ally of Hamas, appeared to be opening a second front in the conflict. This development stretched Israel's military resources even further and raised fears of a wider regional conflagration.

Trey's On-the-Ground Reporting

As these events unfolded, Trey Yingst found himself racing towards the epicenter of the chaos. His journey south from Jerusalem, which began in the early morning hours, quickly turned into a firsthand encounter with the unfolding tragedy.

Arrival in Ashkelon

Trey and his team reached Ashkelon, a coastal city about 8 miles north of the Gaza Strip, shortly after 9 AM. The scene that greeted them was one of confusion and fear. The streets were largely deserted, save for military vehicles and emergency responders rushing to and fro.

As they set up for their first live report from the field, the sound of rocket fire and explosions provided a constant backdrop. Trey, donning his protective vest and helmet, positioned himself with a view of smoke rising from the direction of Gaza.

"I'm Trey Yingst, reporting live from Ashkelon," he began, his voice steady despite the chaos around him. "The situation here is extremely volatile. We've been hearing constant explosions since we arrived. Israeli defense forces are mobilizing, but there's a palpable sense that they've been caught off guard by the scale of this attack."

As he spoke, a loud boom shook the area, causing Trey to instinctively duck. He quickly regained his composure and continued his report. "That explosion you just heard and felt - that's been the reality for residents here all morning. But what's different, what's truly unprecedented, are the reports we're getting of armed militants inside Israeli territory."

Eyewitness Accounts

Between live shots, Trey and his team worked tirelessly to gather more information and eyewitness accounts. They spoke with shocked residents who had fled from communities closer to the Gaza border.

One woman, her voice shaking with emotion, told Trey, "They came into our kibbutz. We could hear gunfire, screaming. We hid in our safe room for hours before we managed to escape. I don't know what's happened to our neighbors, our friends."

Trey listened intently, his expression a mix of empathy and professional focus. He knew that these personal stories would be crucial in helping viewers understand the human impact of the attacks.

Moving Closer to Danger

As the morning wore on, Trey made the decision to push further south, closer to the areas where the fighting was most intense. It was a calculated risk, but one he felt was necessary to truly capture the story.

Their journey took them through checkpoints manned by increasingly tense Israeli soldiers. At each stop, they were warned of the dangers ahead. But Trey was determined to get as close to the events as safely possible.

Reporting from Sderot

By midday, Trey and his team had reached the outskirts of Sderot, one of the hardest-hit towns. The scene was apocalyptic. Plumes of smoke rose from multiple locations within the town. The crack of gunfire could be heard sporadically, indicating that fighting was still ongoing.

Trey set up for another live report, this time with the town of Sderot visible behind him. His voice was grim as he described what he was seeing. "The town of Sderot, which has long lived under the threat of rocket fire from Gaza, is now a battlefield. We can see Israeli forces engaged in firefights with militants who have infiltrated the town. The residents here are trapped, many hiding in shelters, as this unthinkable scenario plays out in their streets."

As he spoke, a group of Israeli soldiers rushed past, taking up positions nearby. The immediacy of the danger was clear, but Trey continued his report, providing viewers with a raw, unfiltered look at the unfolding crisis.

Documenting the Human Cost

Between broadcasts, Trey and his team worked to document the human cost of the attacks. They interviewed paramedics who described scenes of carnage in the communities they'd responded to. They spoke with distraught family members searching for information about loved ones.

One interview particularly stood out. Trey spoke with a young man who had escaped the Nova music festival. The survivor, still in shock, recounted the horrifying moments when the attack began. "We were dancing, celebrating life, and then suddenly... death was all around us. People falling, screaming, trying to run. I can't believe I made it out."

Trey listened, offering words of comfort while ensuring that this crucial testimony was recorded. He knew that these personal stories would be essential in helping the world understand the true impact of the day's events.

Balancing Reporting and Safety

Throughout the morning, Trey had to constantly balance his drive to report the story with the very real dangers present. There were several moments when he and his team had to quickly take cover as rocket sirens wailed or gunfire erupted nearby.

During one particularly close call, as they sheltered behind their vehicle while rockets flew overhead, Trey turned to his cameraman Jake. "You okay?" he asked, concern evident in his voice. Jake nodded grimly, his hand steady on the camera despite the danger. This moment of shared experience, of facing danger together in pursuit of the story, highlighted the bond between the members of Trey's team.

Providing Context and Analysis

As the morning turned to afternoon, Trey's reporting began to shift from purely descriptive to more analytical. Drawing on his years of experience covering the region, he started to provide context for the events unfolding around him.

In one report, standing against the backdrop of Israeli tanks moving towards Gaza, Trey explained, "What we're seeing today represents a catastrophic intelligence failure on the part of Israel. The scale and coordination of this attack suggest long-term planning by Hamas. The question now is how Israel will respond, and what this means for the future of the region."

These moments of analysis, delivered from the heart of the conflict zone, showcased Trey's ability to go beyond mere reporting of facts to provide viewers with a deeper understanding of the significance of the events.

The Toll of Reporting

As the intensity of the morning's events began to take their toll, Trey found moments to reflect on what he was witnessing. During a brief lull between reports, he sat in the team's vehicle, his head in his hands. The weight of the tragedy he was documenting was palpable.

Mira, the local producer, placed a hand on his shoulder. "You're doing important work, Trey," she said softly. "The world needs to see this."

Trey looked up, his eyes reflecting a mix of exhaustion and determination. "I know," he replied. "It's just... I've covered conflicts before, but this... this is different."

This moment of vulnerability, quickly pushed aside as they moved to their next location, highlighted the personal cost of bearing witness to such traumatic events.

The Morning Ends, The Story Continues

As the morning hours came to an end, the full scale of the October 7th attacks was becoming clear. But for Trey Yingst and his team, the day was far from over. The chaos that had erupted at dawn showed no signs of abating.

Trey's final report of the morning came from a hilltop overlooking Gaza. Smoke rose from multiple locations in the Strip, evidence of Israeli retaliatory strikes. But the focus remained on the unprecedented events within Israel itself.

"As we move into the afternoon hours," Trey reported, his voice carrying the weight of all he had witnessed, "the situation remains highly volatile.

Israeli forces are now mounting a significant counteroffensive, but many areas remain unsecured. The death toll, while still unconfirmed, is expected to be high. And perhaps most disturbingly, we're hearing reports of numerous civilians taken hostage and brought into Gaza."

He paused, looking directly into the camera, his expression somber. "In all my years covering this region, I've never seen anything like what I've witnessed this morning. And I fear that the worst may be yet to come."

As the camera cut away, Trey turned to his team. There was no time to rest. The biggest story of their careers was unfolding around them, and they knew their work was far from done. With determination etched on their faces, they packed up their equipment and prepared to head to their next location. The afternoon of October 7th, with all its horrors and challenges, awaited.

8. Afternoon: The Scale Becomes Clear

Ongoing Attacks and Responses

As the sun reached its zenith over Israel on October 7th, 2023, the full scale of the Hamas attack was becoming horrifyingly clear. What had begun as a shocking surprise assault at dawn had evolved into a sustained, multi-pronged offensive that was stretching Israel's defenses to their limits.

Continued Fighting in Border Communities

Throughout the afternoon, fierce fighting continued in the Israeli communities near the Gaza border. The towns of Sderot, Netivot, and Ofakim, as well as numerous kibbutzim, remained under threat. Israeli security forces, now fully mobilized, engaged in intense firefights with Hamas militants who had entrenched themselves in these areas.

Trey Yingst, positioned on the outskirts of Sderot, provided regular updates on the situation. "The sounds of gunfire and explosions have been constant," he reported during one live broadcast. "Israeli forces are going house to house, trying to clear out militants and rescue civilians. But the process is slow and dangerous."

Hostage Crisis Unfolds

One of the most distressing aspects of the afternoon's developments was the emerging hostage crisis. Reports began to flood in of Israeli civilians, including women, children, and the elderly, being taken captive and transported into Gaza.

Trey's team managed to interview a resident of Kibbutz Nir Oz who had narrowly escaped abduction. The man, visibly shaken, recounted how he had watched helplessly as his neighbors were loaded into vehicles by armed militants. "They took entire families," he said, his voice breaking. "We don't know where they are or what will happen to them."

This testimony, broadcast live, brought home the human cost of the attack in a way that statistics couldn't. Trey's empathetic yet professional handling of the interview showcased his ability to balance sensitivity with the need to inform the public.

Israeli Military Response Intensifies

As the afternoon progressed, the Israeli military's response began to gain momentum. The initial shock of the morning attack gave way to a determined counteroffensive.

From his vantage point near the Gaza border, Trey observed and reported on the massive mobilization of Israeli forces. "We're seeing a constant stream of military vehicles heading towards Gaza," he noted during one broadcast. "Tanks, armored personnel carriers, and infantry units are all moving into position. The Israeli Air Force is also intensifying its strikes on targets within Gaza."

The sky above was filled with the contrails of Iron Dome interceptors as they worked to knock down the continuing barrage of rockets from Gaza. The deep booms of artillery fire provided a constant backdrop to Trey's reports.

Expansion of the Conflict

As the afternoon wore on, there were signs that the conflict was expanding beyond the immediate Gaza border region. Reports came in of rocket strikes as far north as Tel Aviv and Jerusalem. Trey's producer, Mira, was constantly on the phone, gathering information from her network of contacts across the country.

"We're hearing that Hezbollah may be increasing its involvement from the north," Mira informed Trey between broadcasts. "There have been exchanges of fire along the Lebanese border."

This information added a new dimension to Trey's reporting. He began to analyze the potential for the conflict to escalate into a wider regional war, drawing on his deep knowledge of Middle Eastern geopolitics.

International Reactions

As the afternoon progressed, international reactions to the attacks began to pour in. World leaders condemned the Hamas assault and expressed support for Israel. Trey made sure to include these developments in his reports, providing context on how the international community's response might shape the conflict.

"The U.S. has pledged its full support to Israel," Trey reported. "Meanwhile, several Arab states that have normalized relations with Israel are in a difficult position, balancing their recent agreements with traditional support for the Palestinian cause."

Challenges of Reporting Amidst the Chaos

Covering the events of October 7th presented Trey and his team with some of the most significant challenges of their careers. The rapidly evolving situation, combined with the very real dangers on the ground, tested their skills, courage, and ethical standards to the limit.

Navigating Dangerous Territory

One of the most immediate challenges was the physical danger inherent in reporting from an active conflict zone. Trey and his team had to constantly assess and reassess the risks as they moved from location to location.

During one particularly tense moment, as they were attempting to reach a kibbutz that had been attacked, they found themselves caught in a firefight between Israeli forces and Hamas militants. Trey and his cameraman, Jake, were forced to take cover behind their vehicle as bullets whistled overhead.

"We're okay, we're okay," Trey assured his viewers as they broadcast live from their precarious position. "But this gives you an idea of the dangers faced by residents and responders in this area."

This ability to continue reporting while under fire demonstrated Trey's composure and commitment to getting the story, but it also highlighted the extreme risks journalists were taking to cover the events.

Verifying Information

In the chaos of the ongoing attacks, separating fact from rumor became an enormous challenge. Social media was awash with unverified claims and graphic videos, while official sources were often slow to confirm information.

Trey and his team had to work tirelessly to verify every piece of information before including it in their reports. This often meant cross-referencing multiple sources, reaching out to contacts on the ground, and sometimes simply waiting for confirmation even as competing news outlets ran with unverified stories.

"We're hearing reports of an attack on another border community," Trey said during one broadcast. "But I want to stress that we have not yet been able to independently verify this information. We're working to confirm the details and will update you as soon as we can do so reliably."

This commitment to accuracy, even at the cost of being first with a story, was a hallmark of Trey's reporting throughout the day.

Ethical Considerations

The events of October 7th presented numerous ethical challenges for Trey and his team. They had to balance the public's right to know with the need to protect operational security and the privacy of victims.

One particularly difficult moment came when they encountered a group of civilians fleeing from a kibbutz that had been attacked. The refugees were distraught, some were injured, and they begged Trey not to film them for fear that it might endanger family members still trapped in the kibbutz.

Trey made the decision to respect their wishes, turning off the cameras and instead offering what help he could. This choice, prioritizing human dignity over a potential scoop, spoke volumes about Trey's ethical standards as a journalist.

Technical Difficulties

The ongoing conflict presented numerous technical challenges for Trey and his team. Power outages in many areas made it difficult to keep equipment charged. The heavy use of cell networks by emergency services and civilians trying to contact loved ones often made it hard to establish connections for live broadcasts.

Jake, the cameraman, had to be incredibly resourceful, at one point rigging up a makeshift antenna to boost their signal strength. Trey, meanwhile, often had to rely on satellite phones to communicate with his producers when cell networks were down.

Despite these challenges, they managed to provide consistent coverage throughout the afternoon, a testament to their preparation and adaptability.

Emotional Toll

Perhaps the most significant challenge of the day was the emotional toll of witnessing and reporting on such traumatic events. Trey, known for his composure under pressure, found himself deeply affected by the scenes of destruction and human suffering he encountered.

During a rare quiet moment between broadcasts, Trey was seen sitting alone, his head in his hands. When Mira approached to check on him, he looked up, his eyes red-rimmed. "How do you put this into words?" he asked quietly. "How do you convey the scale of this tragedy?"

This moment of vulnerability, quickly pushed aside as they moved to their next location, highlighted the personal cost of bearing witness to such events. It was a reminder that behind the professional exterior, journalists covering conflicts are human beings grappling with the weight of the stories they tell.

Maintaining Objectivity

As an American journalist covering a conflict with deep historical roots and passionate supporters on both sides, Trey faced the challenge of maintaining objectivity in his reporting. This became particularly difficult as the scale of the attacks on Israeli civilians became clear.

Trey worked hard to provide context and multiple perspectives in his reports, even as he documented the immediate aftermath of the Hamas attacks. He included information on the long-standing grievances of Palestinians in Gaza, the history of the conflict, and the potential long-term implications of the day's events.

"What we're seeing today is a horrific attack on Israeli civilians," Trey reported. "But it's important to understand the broader context of the Israeli-Palestinian conflict. The situation in Gaza, with its economic blockade and periodic military confrontations, has created conditions that Hamas has exploited."

This commitment to providing a fuller picture, even in the midst of a shocking attack, demonstrated Trey's dedication to journalistic integrity.

As the afternoon wore on and the scale of the October 7th attacks became increasingly clear, Trey Yingst continued to report from the heart of the conflict zone. His coverage, marked by courage, empathy, and a commitment to truth, would prove instrumental in helping the world understand the events of this dark day in Middle Eastern history.

The sun was now beginning its descent towards the horizon, but for Trey and his team, and for the people of Israel and Gaza, the long night of October

7th was far from over. The evening would bring new challenges, new horrors, and a deepening understanding of how this day would reshape the region and the world.

9. Evening: A Nation in Shock

Summarizing the Day's Events

As the sun began to set on October 7th, 2023, Israel found itself grappling with a new reality. The day that had begun with a surprise attack had unfolded into one of the most traumatic events in the nation's history. As darkness fell, Trey Yingst and his team faced the daunting task of summarizing the day's events for a world struggling to comprehend the scale of what had transpired.

The Attack

The Hamas assault had begun at dawn with an unprecedented barrage of rockets launched from Gaza. This initial attack was followed by a coordinated ground invasion, with militants breaching the heavily fortified Gaza border fence at multiple points. The attackers, using a combination of motorcycles, pickup trucks, and even paragliders, had quickly spread out across southern Israel.

Civilian Targets

Throughout the day, reports had emerged of attacks on civilian communities near the Gaza border. Towns like Sderot, Netivot, and Ofakim, as well as numerous kibbutzim, had been targeted. The Nova music festival near Kibbutz Re'im had been the site of a particularly horrific massacre, with hundreds of young attendees killed or taken hostage.

Military Response

The Israeli military, initially caught off guard by the scale and coordination of the attack, had spent the day mobilizing a massive response. By evening, substantial forces had been deployed to the Gaza border, and intense fighting was ongoing in several locations. The Israeli Air Force had conducted numerous strikes on targets within Gaza, while ground forces worked to secure compromised areas within Israel.

Hostage Situation

One of the most distressing aspects of the attack was the large number of Israeli civilians taken hostage. By evening, it was clear that Hamas militants had managed to transport scores of captives back into Gaza. This development added a new layer of complexity to Israel's potential response.

Casualties

As night fell, the full extent of the casualties was still unclear. However, preliminary reports suggested that the death toll on the Israeli side was in the hundreds, with thousands more injured. The number of Palestinian casualties, both from the initial attack and subsequent Israeli retaliation, was also significant but harder to verify.

Wider Implications

The events of October 7th had implications far beyond the immediate conflict zone. There were concerns about potential escalation, particularly along Israel's northern border with Lebanon. The international community had spent the day issuing statements of support for Israel and condemnation of the attacks, but questions remained about how this would translate into action.

Trey's Broadcasts and Their Impact

Throughout this long and harrowing day, Trey Yingst had been a constant presence on Fox News, providing viewers around the world with real-time updates and analysis. As evening approached, his role shifted from reporting on unfolding events to helping make sense of what had transpired.

The 7 PM Broadcast

At 7 PM local time, Trey delivered what would become one of his most impactful broadcasts of the day. Standing on a hilltop overlooking Gaza, with the sound of ongoing fighting in the background, he began his summary of the day's events.

"Good evening. I'm Trey Yingst, reporting from southern Israel. Behind me, you can see the Gaza Strip, from where today's unprecedented attack was launched. What we've witnessed over the past 14 hours is nothing short of a catastrophe."

Trey then proceeded to give a detailed account of the day's events, drawing on everything he and his team had seen and reported throughout the day. He described the initial rocket barrage, the breach of the border, and the attacks on civilian communities. His voice, steady throughout the day, now carried a weight that reflected the gravity of what he was reporting.

"The scenes we've encountered today will haunt this region for years to come," he said. "We've seen communities devastated, families torn apart, and a nation left reeling. The full scale of this tragedy is still emerging, but it's clear that this is one of the darkest days in Israel's history."

Personal Testimonies

One of the most powerful aspects of Trey's evening broadcasts was his inclusion of personal testimonies from those he'd encountered throughout the day. He recounted the stories of survivors from the Nova music festival, of families who'd hidden for hours as militants roamed their communities, and of first responders who'd witnessed unspeakable horrors.

These personal accounts, delivered with empathy but without sensationalism, brought home the human cost of the day's events in a way that statistics alone could not. Viewers around the world found themselves connecting with the individual stories of loss and survival, gaining a deeper understanding of the impact of the attack.

Analysis and Context

As he had done throughout the day, Trey continued to provide analysis and context in his evening reports. He explained the historical background of the Israeli-Palestinian conflict, the recent developments that may have contributed to the attack, and the potential ramifications for the region.

"What we're seeing here is not just a military conflict," Trey explained. "It's a seismic event that will reshape the political landscape of the Middle East. The repercussions of today's attack will be felt far beyond Israel and Gaza."

This ability to zoom out and provide a broader perspective, even while reporting from the heart of the conflict zone, set Trey's coverage apart and helped viewers grasp the wider significance of the day's events.

Challenging Official Narratives

Throughout the evening, Trey continued to demonstrate his commitment to journalistic integrity by challenging official narratives and asking tough questions. In one notable exchange, he pressed an Israeli military spokesperson on how Hamas had managed to breach the border defenses so comprehensively.

"With all due respect," Trey said, "this attack represents a massive intelligence and security failure. How can Israeli citizens trust that they'll be protected going forward?"

This willingness to ask difficult questions, even in the midst of a national tragedy, earned Trey respect from viewers and fellow journalists alike.

The Human Side of Reporting

As the evening wore on, Trey's broadcasts began to reveal the toll that the day's events had taken on him and his team. In one unguarded moment, caught between segments, viewers saw Trey slump against a wall, exhaustion etched on his face. When the camera returned to him, he was once again the consummate professional, but that brief glimpse of vulnerability served as a reminder of the human beings behind the news reports.

Later in the evening, during a live segment, Trey's voice cracked slightly as he described a particularly harrowing encounter with a family searching for their missing daughter. He paused, took a deep breath, and continued. This moment of emotion, quickly controlled but deeply felt, resonated with viewers and highlighted the empathy that characterized Trey's reporting.

Impact of the Coverage

The impact of Trey's broadcasts throughout the day, and particularly in the evening hours, was significant. His on-the-ground reporting provided viewers with an unfiltered look at the unfolding crisis, while his analysis helped contextualize the events within the broader regional dynamics.

Social media was flooded with clips from Trey's reports, with many praising his bravery, professionalism, and insight. Journalists from other networks cited his coverage, and his reports were referenced in official statements and press briefings.

Perhaps most importantly, Trey's reporting helped shape the global understanding of the October 7th attacks. His clear, factual accounts cut through the fog of misinformation that often surrounds such events, while his empathetic approach to telling individual stories humanized the conflict in a way that resonated with viewers around the world.

The Midnight Broadcast

As October 7th drew to a close, Trey delivered what would be his final broadcast of this long and tragic day. Standing in the same spot where he'd begun his reporting in the early morning hours, Trey looked visibly exhausted but remained focused.

"It's now midnight here in Israel," he began. "In the 18 hours since Hamas launched its attack, we've witnessed events that will reshape this region for years to come. The death toll continues to rise, with current estimates suggesting hundreds of Israeli civilians have been killed. An unknown number of hostages have been taken into Gaza. The Israeli military response is ongoing and intensifying."

He paused, looking directly into the camera. "But numbers and strategic analyses can't fully capture what we've seen today. We've witnessed communities shattered, lives destroyed, a nation left in shock. The road ahead is uncertain, but one thing is clear: October 7th, 2023, will be remembered as a day that changed everything in this long-troubled region."

As the broadcast ended and the camera switched off, Trey turned to his team. They exchanged weary glances, each understanding that while their long day was ending, the story they had covered was far from over. The impact of October 7th would continue to unfold in the days, weeks, and months to come, and Trey Yingst would be there to report on it all.

The day that had begun with the wail of sirens at dawn had ended in a nation forever changed. Trey Yingst, through his tireless reporting, had helped the world understand the magnitude of what had transpired. As he finally allowed himself to rest, he knew that the events of this black Saturday would stay with him, and with the world, for a long time to come.

Part IV: Immediate Aftermath

10. The Day After

Assessing the Damage

As the sun rose on October 8th, 2023, it illuminated a changed Israel. The nation that had gone to sleep on Friday night, preparing for a peaceful Sabbath, had awakened on Saturday to a nightmare. Now, as a new day dawned, the full extent of the damage began to come into focus.

Physical Destruction

The border regions near Gaza bore the brunt of the physical damage. Towns like Sderot, Ashkelon, and Netivot showed signs of intense fighting. Buildings were pockmarked with bullet holes, streets were littered with debris, and in some areas, structures had been completely destroyed by rocket fire or deliberate demolition by the militants.

In the kibbutzim closest to the Gaza border, the destruction was even more severe. Some communities, like Kfar Aza and Be'eri, had been all but razed to the ground. The carefully tended gardens and communal spaces that had once defined these tight-knit communities were now scenes of devastation.

Human Toll

As emergency services and military personnel continued their grim work, the human cost of the attack became clearer. Hospitals across southern and central Israel were overwhelmed with the injured. Temporary morgues had been set up to deal with the unprecedented number of fatalities.

By midday on October 8th, Israeli authorities released preliminary casualty figures that shocked the nation and the world. Over 700 Israelis were confirmed dead, with the number expected to rise as more areas were secured and searched. Thousands more were injured, many critically.

The number of hostages taken into Gaza remained unclear, but estimates suggested it could be in the hundreds. Families across Israel anxiously awaited news of missing loved ones, hoping they would be found alive but fearing the worst.

Military Situation

The Israeli Defense Forces (IDF) had spent the night consolidating their positions and pushing remaining Hamas militants out of Israeli territory. By morning, they declared that they had regained control of all breached areas, though sporadic fighting continued in some locations.

The focus was now shifting to Gaza itself. The Israeli Air Force had conducted numerous strikes overnight, targeting Hamas infrastructure and leadership. On the ground, tanks and troops were massing along the border, fueling speculation about a potential ground invasion.

National Mood

The mood across Israel was one of shock, grief, and anger. The nation that had prided itself on its strong defenses and intelligence capabilities was grappling with how such a catastrophic attack could have occurred.

Flags flew at half-mast across the country. Radio and television stations played somber music, interrupted frequently by news updates and lists of the dead and missing. In cities far from the conflict zone, people gathered in squares and at impromptu memorials, lighting candles and saying prayers for the victims.

International Reactions

As the world awoke to the full scale of what had happened in Israel, international reactions poured in. World leaders universally condemned the Hamas attack and expressed solidarity with Israel. Many countries offered humanitarian aid and assistance in locating hostages.

However, questions were already being raised about the potential Israeli response and its implications for regional stability. There were concerns about the possibility of a wider conflict, particularly given the tensions along the Lebanon border and the potential for Iranian involvement.

Trey's Continued Reporting

For Trey Yingst, there was no respite. After a few hours of fitful sleep in a makeshift camp near the Gaza border, he was back on air, bringing the world the latest developments and helping to make sense of the evolving situation.

Dawn Broadcast

Trey's first broadcast on October 8th came just as the sun was rising. Standing amidst the rubble of a bombed-out building in Sderot, he painted a vivid picture of the destruction around him.

"Good morning. I'm Trey Yingst, reporting from Sderot, Israel. The scene here is one of utter devastation. This building behind me, once a family home, is now a pile of concrete and twisted metal. And this is just one small part of the widespread destruction we're seeing across southern Israel this morning."

As he spoke, the camera panned across the street, showing more damaged buildings and debris-strewn roads. In the distance, plumes of smoke could be seen rising from the direction of Gaza, evidence of ongoing Israeli airstrikes.

Eyewitness Accounts

Throughout the morning, Trey sought out survivors and eyewitnesses, bringing their stories to a global audience. One particularly moving interview was with a young woman who had escaped the Nova music festival attack.

"We were dancing, celebrating life," she said, her voice shaking. "And then... death was everywhere. I saw my friends gunned down. I ran and hid in the bushes for hours. I still can't believe I'm alive."

Trey listened intently, his expression a mix of empathy and professional focus. He knew that these personal stories were crucial in helping the world understand the human impact of the attack.

Challenging Questions

As the day progressed, Trey's reporting began to ask harder questions. In an interview with an Israeli military spokesman, he pressed for answers on how the attack had been allowed to happen.

"The scale of this attack suggests a massive intelligence failure," Trey said. "How did Hamas manage to plan and execute such a coordinated assault without detection?"

The spokesman's answers were vague, highlighting the ongoing state of shock within the Israeli establishment. Trey's willingness to ask tough questions, even in the midst of national trauma, underscored his commitment to thorough, unbiased reporting.

On the Gaza Border

By midday, Trey had made his way to a hilltop overlooking the Gaza Strip. From this vantage point, he could see Israeli forces massing along the border and hear the constant thump of artillery fire.

"The question now is what comes next," Trey reported. "The Israeli military is clearly preparing for a major operation. But with hundreds of hostages believed to be in Gaza, any large-scale assault carries enormous risks."

As he spoke, the sound of jets could be heard overhead, followed by explosions in the distance. Trey's ability to provide context and analysis while reporting from the heart of an active conflict zone showcased his skill and experience as a war correspondent.

Humanitarian Crisis

As the day wore on, Trey turned his attention to the growing humanitarian crisis. He visited a hospital in Ashkelon, where staff were struggling to cope with the influx of injured.

"The scenes here are heartbreaking," Trey reported from outside the emergency room. "Doctors and nurses have been working non-stop for over 24 hours. They're running low on supplies, especially blood. And still, ambulances keep arriving with more wounded."

His report highlighted not just the immediate impact of the attack, but the ongoing challenges faced by the healthcare system and first responders.

Political Fallout

By evening, Trey was reporting on the political ramifications of the attack. He secured an interview with a member of the Israeli opposition, who criticized the government's handling of the crisis.

"This is a failure of leadership," the politician said. "We need a unity government to deal with this crisis. The time for political squabbles is over."

Trey's coverage of the political aspects of the crisis provided viewers with a comprehensive understanding of how the events of October 7th were reshaping Israeli society and politics.

Personal Reflections

As night fell on October 8th, Trey delivered what would become one of his most memorable broadcasts of the crisis. Standing in the ruins of Kibbutz Be'eri, surrounded by destruction, he offered a personal reflection on what he had witnessed.

"I've covered conflicts and disasters around the world," he began, his voice heavy with emotion. "But I've never seen anything like this. The scale of the destruction, the depth of the trauma inflicted on this nation... it's almost beyond comprehension."

He paused, collecting himself. "As a journalist, my job is to report the facts, to help people understand what's happening here. But there are moments when facts and figures feel inadequate. How do you quantify grief? How do you measure the loss of security, of innocence, that this nation has experienced?"

Trey's willingness to share his personal struggle to make sense of what he was reporting resonated deeply with viewers. It humanized the news in a way that raw facts and figures could not, helping people around the world connect with the reality of what had happened in Israel.

The Road Ahead

As Trey wrapped up his reporting on October 8th, he turned his attention to what lay ahead. In his final broadcast of the day, he outlined the challenges facing Israel and the wider region.

"The immediate crisis may be over," he said, "but the repercussions of October 7th will be felt for years to come. Israel faces difficult decisions about how to respond. The fate of the hostages hangs in the balance. And the broader implications for regional stability remain uncertain."

He concluded with a somber prediction: "Whatever happens next, it's clear that October 7th, 2023, has changed the Middle East irrevocably. The road ahead will be long and fraught with danger. And we'll be here to report on every step of that journey."

As the camera cut away, Trey slumped against a nearby wall, the exhaustion of two days of non-stop reporting finally catching up with him. But even in his fatigue, his mind was already turning to the stories that needed to be told tomorrow, and in the days and weeks to come.

The events of October 7th and their immediate aftermath had challenged Trey Yingst as a journalist and as a human being. His reporting had helped the world understand the magnitude of what had happened in Israel. Now, as the crisis entered a new phase, Trey knew that his work was far from over. The story of October 7th, and its long-lasting impacts, was just beginning to unfold.

11. Global Reactions

International Responses

The events of October 7th, 2023, sent shockwaves far beyond the borders of Israel and Gaza. As news of the Hamas attack spread, world leaders, international organizations, and citizens across the globe reacted with a mix of horror, condemnation, and concern for the future of the region.

United States

The response from Israel's closest ally was swift and unequivocal. President Biden addressed the nation from the Oval Office within hours of the attack, strongly condemning Hamas and pledging support for Israel.

"The United States stands with Israel," Biden declared. "This attack on innocent civilians is an act of pure evil. We will provide whatever support Israel needs to defend itself and its people."

The President's words were quickly followed by action. The Pentagon announced the deployment of an aircraft carrier group to the eastern Mediterranean, a clear signal of U.S. military support. Additionally, emergency aid packages were prepared, including military supplies and humanitarian assistance.

European Union

The European Union, often divided on issues related to the Israeli-Palestinian conflict, presented a largely united front in the wake of October 7th. European Commission President Ursula von der Leyen issued a statement condemning the attacks and expressing solidarity with Israel.

"The EU stands with Israel in this dark hour," von der Leyen stated. "Hamas's actions are unjustifiable and must be universally condemned."

However, some differences in tone were evident among EU member states. While countries like Germany and France offered unqualified support for Israel, others, such as Ireland and Sweden, while condemning the attacks, also expressed concern about the potential for escalation and urged restraint in Israel's response.

United Nations

The United Nations Security Council convened an emergency session on October 8th to address the crisis. Secretary-General António Guterres issued a statement condemning the Hamas attack and calling for an immediate de-escalation.

"I am appalled by the attacks on Israeli civilians," Guterres said. "At the same time, I am deeply concerned about the potential for a wider conflict. I call on all parties to exercise maximum restraint and to protect civilian lives."

The Security Council, however, found itself deadlocked. A resolution condemning the attacks and calling for the immediate release of hostages was vetoed by Russia, which argued for a more "balanced" approach that would also address longstanding Palestinian grievances.

Arab World

Reactions from Arab countries were notably mixed. Nations that had normalized relations with Israel through the Abraham Accords, such as the United Arab Emirates and Bahrain, found themselves in a delicate position. While they condemned the attacks on civilians, their statements were generally more muted compared to Western responses.

Egypt, which shares a border with both Israel and Gaza, took on a mediating role almost immediately. President Abdel Fattah el-Sisi offered to facilitate negotiations for a ceasefire and the release of hostages.

In contrast, Iran, a longtime supporter of Hamas, stopped short of explicitly endorsing the attack but praised what it called Palestinian resistance against Israeli occupation. This stance heightened concerns about the potential for the conflict to spread beyond Gaza.

Russia and China

The responses from these two global powers were carefully calibrated. Both countries condemned violence against civilians but avoided singling out Hamas for criticism. Instead, they called for a return to negotiations and a two-state solution. Russian President Vladimir Putin, in a statement, emphasized the need for a "comprehensive and lasting settlement" to the Israeli-Palestinian conflict. Chinese Foreign Minister Wang Yi echoed this sentiment, urging "all parties to remain calm and exercise restraint."

These measured responses reflected the complex geopolitical calculations at play, as both Russia and China sought to balance their relationships in the Middle East and their positions on the global stage.

Global Public Opinion

Beyond official government responses, the October 7th attacks sparked intense public reactions worldwide. Social media platforms were flooded with expressions of solidarity with Israel, using hashtags like #StandWithIsrael. At the same time, pro-Palestinian voices emphasized the broader context of the Israeli-Palestinian conflict.

149

Demonstrations were held in major cities around the world. In New York, London, and Paris, thousands gathered to show support for Israel. Meanwhile, in cities with large Arab or Muslim populations, there were protests against potential Israeli retaliation and in support of Palestinian rights.

The global public reaction highlighted the deep divisions and passionate feelings that the Israeli-Palestinian conflict continues to evoke around the world.

Media Coverage Analysis

The October 7th attacks and their aftermath dominated global media coverage for days. News organizations worldwide scrambled to provide comprehensive reporting on the unfolding crisis. However, the coverage itself became a subject of scrutiny and debate.

Immediate Coverage

In the initial hours of the attack, most major news outlets relied heavily on Israeli sources and eyewitness accounts. The shocking nature of the events led to some sensationalist headlines, with terms like "bloodbath" and "massacre" appearing frequently.

CNN's Wolf Blitzer, reporting live from Washington, captured the tone of much of the early coverage: "What we're seeing in Israel is unprecedented. The scale of this attack is unlike anything we've witnessed in recent history."

Challenges in Verification

As the day progressed, news organizations faced significant challenges in verifying information. The chaotic nature of the events, coupled with the flood of often graphic videos and images on social media, made fact-checking difficult.

The BBC's Middle East editor, Jeremy Bowen, addressed this issue directly in one broadcast: "We're seeing a lot of disturbing footage circulating online. We're working to verify these videos before we include them in our reporting. It's a challenging process, but accuracy is paramount."

Criticism of Initial Response

Some media outlets faced criticism for what was perceived as a slow initial response to the attacks. The New York Times, in particular, was called out for not immediately updating its front page to reflect the magnitude of the events.

Margaret Sullivan, former public editor of The New York Times, commented on this in a column: "In the age of digital news, readers expect instant updates on major events. The delay in front-page coverage of the October 7th attacks raised questions about news priorities and readiness to respond to fast-moving crises."

Framing of the Conflict

As the immediate shock of the attack gave way to analysis, differences in how media outlets framed the conflict became apparent. Some, particularly in the United States and parts of Europe, focused primarily on the Hamas attack and Israel's right to self-defense.

Fox News, where Trey Yingst's reporting featured prominently, took this approach. One headline read: "Israel Under Siege: Nation Fights Back Against Hamas Terror."

Other outlets, particularly those in the Arab world and some left-leaning Western publications, placed more emphasis on the broader context of the Israeli-Palestinian conflict. Al Jazeera's coverage, for instance, consistently referred to Hamas as a "resistance movement" rather than a terrorist organization.

Coverage of Civilian Casualties

The reporting on civilian casualties became a particularly contentious issue. While the deaths of Israeli civilians were widely and graphically reported, some news organizations were criticized for being less forthcoming about Palestinian civilian casualties resulting from Israel's retaliatory strikes.

Reporters Without Borders issued a statement calling for balanced coverage: "While the horror of the initial attack must be fully reported, it's equally important to document the impact of the conflict on all civilians, regardless of nationality."

Role of Social Media

Social media played a significant role in shaping the narrative around the October 7th attacks. Platforms like Twitter (X) and TikTok were flooded with firsthand accounts, videos, and opinions. This real-time, unfiltered information presented both opportunities and challenges for traditional media.

Emily Bell, director of the Tow Center for Digital Journalism at Columbia University, observed: "The October 7th attacks highlighted both the power and the peril of social media in crisis reporting. While platforms provided immediate, on-the-ground perspectives, they also facilitated the rapid spread of misinformation."

Trey Yingst's Impact

In this complex media landscape, Trey Yingst's reporting stood out for its clarity, depth, and on-the-ground perspective. His live broadcasts from the conflict zone provided viewers with an unfiltered look at the unfolding crisis.

Brian Stelter, former CNN media correspondent, noted: "Yingst's coverage exemplified the value of having experienced correspondents on the ground. His ability to provide context while reporting from the heart of the conflict set a high standard for crisis journalism."

Yingst's reporting was widely shared and cited by other media outlets, contributing significantly to the global understanding of the events of October 7th and their aftermath.

Ethical Debates

The coverage of the October 7th attacks reignited long-standing debates about journalistic ethics in covering conflicts. Questions about the use of graphic imagery, the protection of sources in conflict zones, and the responsibility to provide context were all brought to the fore. The Dart Center for Journalism and Trauma issued guidelines for reporters covering the crisis, emphasizing the need for sensitivity when interviewing victims and the importance of self-care for journalists exposed to traumatic events.

Long-Term Impact on Media Narratives

As the immediate crisis gave way to ongoing conflict, media analysts began to assess the long-term impact of the October 7th attacks on narratives surrounding the Israeli-Palestinian conflict.

Sarah Leah Whitson, executive director of Democracy for the Arab World Now, argued: "The events of October 7th have reshaped the media landscape around the Israeli-Palestinian conflict. The challenge now is to maintain detailed, contextual reporting as the situation evolves."

The October 7th attacks and their aftermath presented a significant challenge to global media.

The need for immediate, accurate reporting had to be balanced with providing context and avoiding sensationalism. As the crisis continued to unfold, journalists like Trey Yingst played a crucial role in helping the world understand the complexities of the situation and its far-reaching implications.

12. Personal Toll

Impact on Civilians and Communities

The October 7th attacks and their aftermath left an indelible mark on the lives of countless individuals and communities across Israel. The sheer scale of the tragedy, coupled with the brutality of the attacks, created a collective trauma that would take years, if not generations, to heal.

Destroyed Lives in Border Communities

The communities near the Gaza border bore the brunt of the Hamas assault. Towns like Sderot, Netivot, and numerous kibbutzim transformed overnight from peaceful residential areas into war zones. The physical destruction was immense, but the human toll was immeasurable.

In Kibbutz Be'eri, one of the hardest-hit communities, the scars ran deep. Families were torn apart, homes destroyed, and the sense of security that had been carefully cultivated over years was shattered in a matter of hours.

The Nova Music Festival Tragedy

The attack on the Nova music festival near Kibbutz Re'im became a symbol of the October 7th tragedy. What began as a celebration of peace and music ended in unimaginable horror. Hundreds of young people, who had gathered to dance and enjoy life, found themselves fleeing for their lives or, tragically, losing them.

Trey interviewed David Cohen, a survivor of the festival, whose haunted expression spoke volumes:

"One moment we were dancing, the next... chaos. People running, screaming. I saw my friends gunned down. I ran and hid in the bushes for hours. The sounds, the sights... they'll never leave me."

The Nova festival attack highlighted the indiscriminate nature of the violence and the targeting of civilians, shocking the conscience of the world.

Hostage Families

For the families of those taken hostage, the October 7th attacks marked the beginning of a nightmare with no end in sight. The uncertainty of their loved ones' fate created a unique form of anguish.

Trey spoke with Rachel Goldberg, whose son Hersh was among those abducted. Her words captured the agony of waiting:

"Every moment is torture. Is he alive? Is he being treated well? Will I ever see him again? These questions consume me. Our lives are on hold until he comes home."

The hostage crisis added a layer of complexity to the personal and national trauma, as families grappled with hope, fear, and the frustration of helplessness.

Psychological Impact

The psychological impact of the attacks extended far beyond those directly affected. Across Israel, a nation accustomed to conflict found itself grappling with a new level of fear and insecurity.

Dr. Yael Levin, a trauma specialist working with survivors, explained to Trey:

"What we're seeing is unprecedented. The scale of the trauma, the brutality of the attacks... it's challenging our existing models of PTSD treatment. We're dealing with not just individual trauma, but collective societal trauma."

Reports of anxiety, depression, and PTSD skyrocketed in the weeks following October 7th. Children, in particular, showed signs of severe stress, with many refusing to leave their homes or sleep alone.

Economic Fallout

The personal toll of the attacks extended to economic hardship for many. Businesses in the affected areas were destroyed or forced to close. Tourism, a significant part of Israel's economy, ground to a halt.

Moshe Azoulay, a small business owner in Ashkelon, told Trey:

"I've lost everything. My shop is gone, and even if I could rebuild, who would come? Our whole community is shattered. How do we come back from this?"

The economic impact added another layer of stress to communities already struggling to cope with the physical and emotional aftermath of the attacks.

Resilience Amidst Tragedy

Despite the overwhelming tragedy, stories of resilience and community spirit emerged. Trey reported on numerous instances of Israelis coming together to support each other, from volunteers distributing food and supplies to therapists offering free counseling services.

In one particularly moving scene, Trey filmed a group of young Israelis cleaning up debris in Sderot, singing as they worked. Their spirit in the face of devastation offered a glimmer of hope amidst the darkness.

Trey's Reflections and Emotional Journey

For Trey Yingst, covering the October 7th attacks and their aftermath was more than just another assignment. It was a profound personal and professional challenge that would leave an indelible mark on his life and career.

Initial Shock and Adrenaline

In the immediate aftermath of the attacks, Trey's professional instincts kicked in. The adrenaline of being in the midst of a breaking news story of global significance initially overshadowed the emotional impact of what he was witnessing.

During a rare quiet moment on October 8th, Trey reflected in his personal journal:

"It's been 24 hours of non-stop reporting. I've seen things I never thought I'd see. The destruction, the loss of life... it's overwhelming. But there's no time to process. The story needs to be told."

This entry captured the conflict many journalists face in crisis situations – the need to report versus the human reaction to tragedy.

Confronting the Human Toll

As the days wore on, the human stories behind the headlines began to weigh heavily on Trey. Each interview with a survivor, each conversation with a grieving family member, chipped away at his professional detachment.

After interviewing a mother who had lost both her children in the Nova festival attack, Trey struggled to maintain his composure on camera. In a later conversation with his producer, he admitted:

"I've covered conflicts before, but this... this feels different. The raw grief, the senselessness of it all. It's getting harder to keep my emotions in check."

This moment of vulnerability highlighted the challenge of balancing professional objectivity with human empathy.

Ethical Dilemmas

Trey found himself grappling with ethical dilemmas throughout his coverage. The need to report the truth clashed at times with concerns about retraumatizing survivors or potentially compromising security.

One particularly difficult decision came when Trey obtained footage of hostages being taken into Gaza. After much deliberation with his team and network executives, he decided not to air the most graphic parts of the video.

In his journal, he wrote:

"The public has a right to know, but at what cost? There's a line between reporting and exploitation. I'm not always sure where that line is, but I know I don't want to cross it."

These ethical considerations added another layer of stress to an already challenging situation.

Physical and Emotional Exhaustion

The relentless pace of reporting, combined with the emotional weight of the stories he was covering, began to take a toll on Trey. By the end of the first week, signs of exhaustion were evident.

During one live broadcast, viewers noticed Trey's hands shaking slightly as he held the microphone. Off-camera, he experienced headaches and difficulty sleeping.

In a text to a colleague back in the U.S., Trey admitted:

"I'm running on fumes. Every time I close my eyes, I see the faces of the people I've interviewed, the destruction I've witnessed. But I can't stop. This story needs to be told."

This dedication to the story, even at personal cost, exemplified Trey's commitment to his profession.

Moments of Connection

Amidst the tragedy, Trey experienced moments of profound human connection that affected him deeply. One such moment came during an interview with an elderly Holocaust survivor who had lost his grandson in the attacks.

The man, after sharing his story, took Trey's hand and said, "Thank you for being here. For telling our stories. It matters."

This simple gesture of gratitude amidst unimaginable grief left a lasting impact on Trey. In his journal that night, he wrote:

"Sometimes, in the midst of all this darkness, you find moments of light. Moments that remind you why we do this job."

These connections helped sustain Trey through the challenging days and weeks of reporting.

Reflections on Journalism's Role

As the immediate crisis gave way to ongoing conflict, Trey began to reflect more deeply on the role of journalism in times of war and tragedy.

In a panel discussion with other war correspondents, Trey shared:

"Our job isn't just to report facts and figures. It's to help people understand, to bear witness, to give voice to those who might otherwise go unheard. But with that comes a huge responsibility. The stories we tell, the words we choose, they matter. They shape how the world understands these events."

This understanding of the weight of his work added depth to Trey's reporting but also increased the pressure he felt.

Personal Growth and Changed Perspectives

The experience of covering the October 7th attacks and their aftermath profoundly changed Trey, both as a journalist and as a person.

In an interview with a journalism school podcast months after the events, Trey reflected:

"I went into October 7th thinking I was prepared for anything. I'd covered conflicts, I'd seen destruction. But nothing could have prepared me for what I witnessed. It's changed how I see the world, how I approach my work, how I understand human resilience and human cruelty."

This personal growth was evident in Trey's subsequent reporting, which showed a deeper empathy and a more nuanced understanding of the complexities of conflict.

Coping and Self-Care

As the weeks of intense coverage turned into months, Trey had to confront the need for self-care and emotional processing. At the urging of his network and colleagues, he began speaking with a therapist experienced in working with journalists in conflict zones.

In his journal, Trey wrote about this experience:

"I resisted at first. Thought I could handle it on my own. But talking to someone who understands what we go through as journalists in these situations... it's helping. Slowly, I'm learning to process what I've seen, what I've felt."

This acknowledgment of the need for mental health support was a significant step for Trey and reflected a growing awareness in the journalism community about the importance of addressing the emotional toll of crisis reporting.

Looking to the Future

As the immediate aftermath of October 7th transitioned into long-term coverage of its repercussions, Trey found himself changed but also reaffirmed in his commitment to journalism.

In his final journal entry included in this chapter, Trey wrote:

"October 7th will always be with me. The stories I've heard, the scenes I've witnessed... they're part of me now. But they've also reinforced why I became a journalist. To shine a light on the darkest corners of human experience, to help people understand, to make sure these stories are not forgotten. The work continues."

This reflection captured the lasting impact of the October 7th attacks on Trey Yingst, both personally and professionally. It marked not an end, but a new chapter in his journey as a journalist, one shaped by the profound experiences of reporting on one of the most significant events in recent Middle Eastern history.

13. Geopolitical Consequences

Shifts in Middle East Dynamics

One of the most immediate and significant shifts occurred among Arab states.

Trey Yingst, reporting from a diplomatic summit in Riyadh just weeks after the attacks, observed:

"There's a palpable tension here. Nations like the UAE and Bahrain, which had been moving closer to Israel, now find themselves in a difficult position. They're trying to balance their strategic interests with the overwhelming public sympathy for Palestinians in Gaza."

This balancing act played out in various ways. While officially condemning the Hamas attacks, many Arab states also criticized Israel's military response in Gaza. The UAE, for instance, called for an immediate ceasefire and increased humanitarian aid to Gaza, while simultaneously reaffirming its commitment to the Abraham Accords.

Iran's Increased Influence

The attacks also served to highlight and potentially increase Iran's influence in the region. As a long-time supporter of Hamas and other militant groups opposed to Israel, Iran found itself at the center of international scrutiny.

In an interview with an Iranian political analyst, Trey probed this issue:

"Some see the October 7th attacks as an extension of Iran's strategy of confrontation with Israel through proxy groups. How do you respond to that?"

The analyst's careful response, emphasizing Iran's support for Palestinian rights while denying direct involvement in the attacks, underscored the delicate diplomatic dance being performed by all parties in the region.

Turkey's Resurgence

Another significant shift came in the form of Turkey's renewed engagement in the Israeli-Palestinian conflict. President Erdogan, who had been working to repair relations with Israel, took a strong stance against Israel's military operation in Gaza.

Trey's report from Istanbul captured this shift:

"President Erdogan's fiery rhetoric, calling Israel's actions in Gaza a 'massacre,' marks a sharp turn from the reconciliation efforts of recent years. Turkey is positioning itself as a champion of the Palestinian cause, potentially altering its relationships not just with Israel, but with other regional powers."

This resurgence of Turkey as a vocal player in the conflict added another layer of complexity to the regional dynamics, potentially impacting everything from diplomatic relations to economic partnerships.

International Diplomatic Efforts

As the conflict intensified, the international community scrambled to respond. Diplomatic efforts took on a new urgency, with various nations and international bodies attempting to mediate, de-escalate, and address the humanitarian crisis unfolding in Gaza.

United States: Walking a Tightrope

The U.S., as Israel's closest ally, found itself in a challenging position. While offering unequivocal support for Israel's right to defend itself, the Biden administration also faced pressure to push for restraint and protect civilian lives in Gaza.

Trey's coverage of U.S. diplomatic efforts highlighted this balancing act. Reporting from outside the U.S. Embassy in Tel Aviv, he noted:

"The U.S. is trying to thread a very fine needle here. They're providing military support to Israel while simultaneously working behind the scenes to moderate the scope of Israel's response. It's a delicate dance that's drawing criticism from both sides of the conflict."

United Nations: Struggles and Stalemates

The United Nations, often seen as the primary forum for international diplomacy, struggled to mount an effective response to the crisis. Multiple attempts to pass resolutions in the Security Council were vetoed, highlighting the deep divisions within the international community.

Trey's report from the UN headquarters in New York captured the frustration:

"The scenes here at the UN are tense. Diplomats are working around the clock, but reaching consensus seems almost impossible. The failure to agree on even a basic humanitarian resolution is being seen by many as a failure of international diplomacy."

Regional Mediation Efforts

Several regional powers stepped up their diplomatic efforts in the wake of the attacks. Egypt, with its unique position as a neighbor to both Israel and Gaza, took on a central role in mediation efforts, particularly in negotiations related to hostages and humanitarian aid.

Qatar, which had long maintained channels of communication with Hamas, also emerged as a key mediator. Trey's interview with a Qatari diplomat shed light on these efforts:

"Our goal is to create a space for dialogue," the diplomat explained. "We're not taking sides, but trying to build bridges that can lead to de-escalation and eventually, we hope, to a lasting peace."

European Union: A United Front?

The European Union sought to present a united front in response to the crisis, but internal divisions quickly became apparent. While all EU nations condemned the Hamas attacks, there were disagreements over the appropriate response to Israel's military operation in Gaza.

Reporting from Brussels, Trey highlighted these tensions:

"The EU is struggling to speak with one voice. While there's unanimous condemnation of the October 7th attacks, we're seeing a split between those calling for unequivocal support for Israel and those pushing for a more balanced approach that also addresses Palestinian grievances."

Long-term Implications for the Region

As the immediate crisis gave way to a prolonged conflict, Trey's reporting began to focus on the long-term implications of the October 7th attacks and their aftermath. These ramifications promised to reshape the Middle East for years, if not decades, to come.

The Future of the Two-State Solution

One of the most significant long-term impacts was on the prospects for a two-state solution to the Israeli-Palestinian conflict. The October 7th attacks and Israel's response in Gaza had deepened mistrust on both sides, making the already difficult path to peace seem even more challenging.

In a special report on the future of peace efforts, Trey interviewed both Israeli and Palestinian peace activists. Their perspectives were sobering:

"The events of October 7th have set us back years, maybe decades," one Israeli activist admitted. "The trauma on both sides is immense. Rebuilding trust will take a monumental effort."

A Palestinian counterpart added: "We've always faced obstacles, but now they seem insurmountable. Yet we have no choice but to keep working for peace. The alternative is endless conflict."

Reshaping of Israeli Society and Politics

The attacks had a profound impact on Israeli society and politics. The sense of vulnerability exposed by the breach of Israel's defenses led to calls for a major overhaul of the country's security apparatus and strategy.

Trey's interviews with Israeli citizens and political figures revealed a nation grappling with its identity and future direction:

"There's a sense that everything has changed," one Israeli politician told Trey. "The old paradigms no longer apply. We're seeing a shift towards more hawkish positions, but also a renewed debate about what true security means in the long term."

The Humanitarian Crisis and Gaza's Future

The extensive damage to Gaza's infrastructure and the loss of civilian life raised serious questions about the territory's future. The humanitarian crisis sparked by the conflict promised to have long-lasting effects on the region's stability and development.

Reporting from the outskirts of Gaza, Trey highlighted the scale of the challenge:

"The destruction we're seeing is almost incomprehensible. Rebuilding Gaza will take years and billions of dollars. But beyond the physical reconstruction, there's the question of how to build a future that doesn't lead back to conflict. That's the real challenge facing not just Gazans, but the entire international community."

Regional Security Architecture

The October 7th attacks exposed vulnerabilities in the regional security architecture, leading to calls for new alliances and defense agreements. Trey's coverage of these developments pointed to a potential reshaping of military and intelligence cooperation in the Middle East.

"We're seeing discussions about new regional security frameworks," a defense analyst explained to Trey. "There's talk of expanded missile defense cooperation, intelligence sharing, and even the possibility of a Middle Eastern version of NATO. The landscape of regional security is being redrawn."

Economic Impacts

The long-term economic implications of the conflict were another focus of Trey's reporting. The war had disrupted trade routes, impacted oil prices, and raised questions about investment in the region.

In a report from Dubai's financial district, Trey explored these issues:

"The October 7th attacks and the subsequent conflict have sent shockwaves through the region's economy. We're seeing a reassessment of risk in many sectors. The push for economic diversification in Gulf states may accelerate as a result, while the rebuilding efforts in Gaza could reshape economic relations in unexpected ways."

The Role of Social Media and Information Warfare

Finally, Trey's reporting highlighted how the conflict had underscored the growing importance of social media and information warfare in modern conflicts. The battle for public opinion, played out on platforms like Twitter and TikTok, had become as important as the physical conflict.

In a special segment on this issue, Trey noted:

"What we're seeing is a war fought on two fronts – one on the ground, and one online. The narratives shaped on social media are influencing public opinion, diplomatic responses, and even military strategy. Understanding and navigating this new landscape of information warfare will be crucial for all parties in future conflicts."

As Trey Yingst continued to report on these long-term implications, he helped his viewers understand that the events of October 7th were not just a momentary crisis, but a turning point that would shape the Middle East for years to come. His in-depth analysis and on-the-ground reporting provided a window into a region in flux, grappling with challenges that would define its future.

The geopolitical consequences of the October 7th attacks were still unfolding, and Trey remained committed to telling this ongoing story. Through his reporting, he continued to bring the complexities of the Middle East to a global audience, helping to foster understanding in a time of profound change and challenge.

Part V: Reflections and Moving Forward

14. Trey Yingst: Personal and Professional Growth

How October 7th Changed His Perspective

A Shattered Sense of Security

One of the most immediate changes in Trey's perspective was a newfound understanding of how quickly a sense of security can be shattered. In an interview six months after the attacks, Trey reflected on this shift:

"I've covered conflicts around the world, but there was always a part of me that believed certain places were 'safe.' October 7th obliterated that notion. It showed how vulnerable we all are, how fragile peace can be."

This realization had a profound impact on Trey's reporting. He began to approach stories with a heightened awareness of underlying tensions and potential flashpoints, even in seemingly stable regions.

The Weight of Bearing Witness

The sheer scale and brutality of the October 7th attacks forced Trey to confront the emotional toll of bearing witness to history's darkest moments. In his personal journal, he wrote:

"I've seen terrible things before, but this was different. The scope of the horror, the intimacy of the violence... it stays with you. I find myself waking up at night, replaying scenes in my head. How do you process something like this? How do you convey it to others without losing a part of yourself?"

This internal struggle led Trey to place greater emphasis on self-care and mental health, both for himself and his team. He became an advocate for better psychological support for journalists covering traumatic events, speaking openly about his own experiences and the importance of addressing the emotional impact of war reporting.

Redefining Objectivity

The October 7th attacks and their aftermath challenged Trey's understanding of journalistic objectivity. He found himself questioning whether true objectivity was possible - or even desirable - in the face of such clear atrocities.

In a panel discussion at the Columbia School of Journalism, Trey said:

"We're taught to be objective, to present both sides. But what does that mean when one side has committed unambiguous war crimes? I've come to believe that objectivity doesn't mean neutrality. It means being fair and accurate, but it also means calling things what they are."

This view of objectivity began to inform Trey's reporting, leading to a style that combined factual accuracy with moral clarity.

The Power and Responsibility of Journalism

October 7th reinforced for Trey the immense power and responsibility that comes with being a journalist in conflict zones. He saw firsthand how his reports could shape public opinion, influence policy decisions, and impact the lives of those caught in the conflict.

In an op-ed for the Columbia Journalism Review, Trey wrote:

"Every word we say, every image we show, carries weight. We're not just reporting news; we're shaping how the world understands these events. That's a tremendous responsibility, and it's one we must approach with the utmost care and consideration."

This realization led Trey to be even more meticulous in his fact-checking and more thoughtful in his choice of words and images. He began to see his role not just as a reporter, but as an educator and interpreter of complex global events.

A Deeper Understanding of the Middle East

While Trey had covered the Middle East extensively before October 7th, the attacks and their aftermath gave him a deeper understanding of the region's complexities. He began to see how historical grievances, religious tensions, and geopolitical maneuvering all intertwined to create the current reality.

In a conversation with a colleague, Trey remarked:

"I thought I understood this region before, but October 7th showed me how much I still had to learn. It's not just about Israel and Palestine anymore. It's about Iran, Turkey, the Gulf states, the U.S., Russia... all these players with their own agendas and interests. And at the center of it all are ordinary people just trying to live their lives."

This deeper understanding began to infuse Trey's reporting with greater context, allowing him to provide viewers with a more comprehensive picture of the region's dynamics.

Impact on His Career Trajectory

The events of October 7th and Trey's coverage of them marked a turning point in his career, cementing his status as one of the leading war correspondents of his generation and opening up new opportunities and challenges.

Recognition and Awards

Trey's reporting on the October 7th attacks and their aftermath earned him widespread recognition within the journalism community. His live broadcasts from the conflict zone, in-depth analysis, and commitment to accuracy in the face of chaos were widely praised.

In the year following the attacks, Trey received several prestigious awards, including the Overseas Press Club Award for best TV spot news reporting and a nomination for an Emmy in the Breaking News category. These accolades not only recognized Trey's work but also raised his profile within the industry.

Expanded Role at Fox News

Trey's performance during the crisis led to an expanded role at Fox News. He was given more latitude in choosing stories to pursue and was increasingly called upon to provide analysis on a wide range of international issues, not just those related to the Middle East.

In a meeting with network executives, Trey was told:

"Your reporting from October 7th showed us and our viewers what truly high-caliber journalism looks like. We want to give you the resources and platform to continue that level of reporting on a global scale."

This vote of confidence translated into more resources for Trey's team and greater editorial input on the network's international coverage.

Book Deal and Speaking Engagements

The intensity and impact of Trey's October 7th coverage led to opportunities beyond broadcast journalism. He was approached by several publishers and eventually signed a deal to write a book about his experiences covering the attacks and their aftermath.

Additionally, Trey became a sought-after speaker at journalism schools, conferences, and think tanks. His firsthand experience and insights into modern conflict reporting made him a valuable voice in discussions about the future of war journalism.

Ethical Leadership

Trey's thoughtful approach to the ethical challenges posed by covering October 7th positioned him as a leader in discussions about journalistic ethics in the digital age. He was invited to join the advisory board of a major journalism ethics institute and began working on developing new guidelines for reporting on traumatic events.

In an address to the institute, Trey said:

"What we experienced and learned from October 7th needs to inform how we approach conflict reporting going forward. We need to balance the public's right to know with our responsibility to minimize harm. We need to find ways to convey the reality of war without becoming purveyors of trauma."

Focus on Long-Form and Investigative Reporting

While Trey continued to cover breaking news, his experiences during and after October 7th sparked a desire to engage in more long-form and investigative reporting. He began working on in-depth pieces that examined the root causes of conflicts and their long-term implications.

In pitching a series of long-form reports to his producers, Trey argued:

"The world's attention span is short. We move from crisis to crisis. But the real stories, the ones that help us understand why these conflicts happen and how we might prevent them, require time and depth. That's the kind of reporting I want to focus on now."

This shift in focus allowed Trey to leverage the insights and connections he had gained during the October 7th crisis to produce more substantive, contextual reporting.

Personal Mission and Legacy

Perhaps the most significant impact on Trey's career trajectory was a shift in how he viewed his personal mission as a journalist. The events of October 7th and their aftermath had shown him the true power of journalism to inform, influence, and potentially even change the course of events.

In a reflective moment during an interview for a journalism podcast, Trey shared:

"Before October 7th, I saw myself as someone who reported the news. Now, I see my role differently.

I'm not just reporting events; I'm helping to shape how we understand our world. That's a huge responsibility, but it's also an incredible opportunity to make a difference."

This newfound sense of purpose began to guide Trey's career decisions, influencing the stories he chose to pursue and the way he approached his reporting. He became more focused on stories that had the potential to drive change or bring attention to overlooked issues.

As Trey moved forward in his career, the lessons and experiences of October 7th continued to inform his work. The perspective he gained during those intense days and weeks became an integral part of his journalistic DNA, shaping his approach to reporting, his ethical standards, and his vision for the future of journalism. The young reporter who had arrived in Israel just days before the attacks had been transformed by the events he witnessed and reported on. Trey Yingst emerged from the crucible of October 7th not just as a more experienced journalist, but as a more thoughtful, empathetic, and purposeful one. His journey, forever altered by that fateful day, was far from over. The story of October 7th and its aftermath had become part of Trey's own story, influencing his path forward and promising to shape his contributions to journalism for years to come.

15. Lessons Learned

For Journalism

The October 7th attacks and their aftermath provided a clear reminder of the critical role journalism plays in times of crisis. Trey Yingst's experiences covering these events yielded valuable lessons for the field of journalism as a whole.

The Importance of On-the-Ground Reporting

One of the most significant takeaways from Trey's coverage was the irreplaceable value of having reporters physically present in conflict zones. In an age of digital communication and remote reporting, the October 7th crisis demonstrated that there is no substitute for firsthand observation and direct engagement with those affected by events.

Trey reflected on this in a panel discussion at the Newseum:

"Being there, smelling the smoke, hearing the sirens, looking into the eyes of survivors – it gives you a perspective that you simply can't get from a satellite feed or a phone interview. It allows you to convey the human reality of a situation in a way that resonates with viewers on a visceral level."

This lesson reinforced the need for news organizations to invest in sending reporters to the scenes of major events, despite the costs and risks involved.

The Challenge of Objectivity in Extreme Situations

The brutal nature of the October 7th attacks forced journalists, including Trey, to grapple with the concept of objectivity in a new way. The traditional notion of presenting "both sides" of a story was challenged by the clear-cut nature of the atrocities committed.

In an article for the Columbia Journalism Review, Trey wrote:

"Objectivity doesn't mean neutrality in the face of evil. It means accurately reporting facts and providing context. In situations like October 7th, we need to find a way to be fair and thorough in our reporting while also clearly conveying the moral weight of events."

This detailed approach to objectivity became a topic of discussion in journalism schools and newsrooms, prompting a reevaluation of how reporters cover conflicts and atrocities.

The Need for Trauma-Informed Reporting

Covering the October 7th attacks exposed Trey and many other journalists to extreme trauma, both directly and through the stories they reported. This experience highlighted the need for better support systems for journalists and more trauma-informed approaches to reporting.

Trey became an advocate for improved mental health resources in newsrooms. He worked with the Dart Center for Journalism and Trauma to develop guidelines for reporting on traumatic events, emphasizing the importance of self-care and ethical treatment of survivors.

"We need to recognize that trauma affects not just those we report on, but also us as journalists," Trey said in a workshop for young reporters. "Learning how to process what we witness and how to interview trauma survivors without causing further harm are essential skills for modern journalists."

Combating Misinformation in Real-Time

The rapid spread of misinformation during and after the October 7th attacks underscored the critical role journalists play in verifying and contextualizing information. Trey's experiences led him to develop new strategies for fact-checking and debunking false narratives in real-time.

He began incorporating regular "fact-check" segments into his reports, directly addressing and correcting misinformation circulating on social media. This approach not only provided accurate information but also educated viewers on how to critically evaluate the news they consume.

"In the age of social media, being first with a story is less important than being right," Trey emphasized in a lecture at Stanford University. "Our credibility is our most valuable asset, and maintaining it requires constant vigilance and a commitment to verification."

For International Relations

The October 7th attacks and their aftermath had far-reaching implications for international relations, offering several crucial lessons for diplomats, policymakers, and global leaders.

The Fragility of Peace Agreements

The sudden eruption of violence on October 7th served as a reminder of the fragility of peace in regions with long-standing conflicts. Despite years of relative calm and even progress towards normalization between Israel and some Arab states, the situation unraveled rapidly.

In an interview with a senior diplomat, Trey explored this theme:

"What we learned on October 7th is that no peace is guaranteed without addressing the root causes of conflict. Surface-level agreements can mask deep-seated grievances that, if left unaddressed, can explode with devastating consequences."

This realization prompted calls for more comprehensive, inclusive approaches to peace-building in conflict zones around the world.

The Interconnectedness of Regional Politics

The October 7th crisis highlighted the intricate web of relationships and interests that connect different actors in the Middle East. What began as a conflict between Israel and Hamas quickly drew in other regional powers, demonstrating the ripple effects of localized conflicts on broader geopolitical dynamics.

Trey's reporting on these interconnections helped viewers understand the complexity of the situation. He explained how events in Gaza could influence politics in Iran, impact oil prices in the Gulf, and affect diplomatic relations between the U.S. and China.

"We can no longer think of conflicts as isolated incidents," Trey noted in a special report. "Every action in this region has the potential to shift the balance of power across multiple countries. Understanding these connections is crucial for effective diplomacy and conflict resolution."

The Role of Non-State Actors

The October 7th attacks demonstrated the significant impact that non-state actors like Hamas can have on international relations. Despite not being recognized as a legitimate government by much of the international community, Hamas's actions reshaped the geopolitical landscape of the entire region.

Trey's coverage explored how this reality challenges traditional approaches to diplomacy and conflict resolution. In a panel discussion with foreign policy experts, he posed the question:

"How do we address conflicts where one of the key actors isn't recognized as a legitimate party by many of the other stakeholders? This is a challenge we're seeing not just in the Middle East, but in conflicts around the world."

This question became a focal point for discussions about the future of international diplomacy and conflict resolution strategies.

The Importance of Rapid, Coordinated International Response

The aftermath of October 7th underscored the need for swift and coordinated international responses to crises. The varying reactions from different countries and international bodies highlighted both the potential and the limitations of global governance structures. Trey's reporting on the

210

international response to the crisis shed light on the complexities of multilateral action. He observed:

"The effectiveness of bodies like the UN Security Council is only as strong as the willingness of member states to find common ground. What we saw after October 7th was a mix of rapid mobilization in some areas and frustrating deadlock in others."

These observations fueled debates about reforming international institutions to better respond to 21st-century crises.

For Humanity

Beyond the realms of journalism and international relations, the October 7th attacks and their aftermath offered profound lessons about human nature, resilience, and the shared challenges facing our global community.

The Persistence of Hate and the Need for Education

The brutality of the October 7th attacks forced a confrontation with the dark realities of hatred and extremism. It raised difficult questions about how such violence could occur in the 21st century and what could be done to prevent it in the future.

In a deeply personal piece written for The Atlantic, Trey reflected:

"What we witnessed on October 7th was not just a military attack, but an assault on the very idea of shared humanity. It forces us to ask: How do we combat the kind of hatred that allows people to commit such acts? The answer, I believe, lies in education, dialogue, and a commitment to seeing the humanity in those we consider 'other.'"

This perspective led to renewed calls for investment in peace education and cross-cultural understanding programs.

The Resilience of the Human Spirit

Amidst the horror and tragedy of October 7th and its aftermath, Trey also witnessed countless examples of human resilience, compassion, and hope. His reporting highlighted stories of survivors helping each other, of communities coming together in the face of adversity, and of individuals working tirelessly for peace despite overwhelming odds.

One particularly moving story Trey covered was that of a mixed Israeli-Palestinian family who, despite losing members to the violence, continued to advocate for coexistence. Trey remarked in his report:

"In the darkest moments, we often see the best of humanity shine through. These stories of resilience and compassion aren't just inspiring – they're a roadmap for how we can move forward from tragedy."

These narratives of resilience became a cornerstone of Trey's reporting, offering glimmers of hope amidst the devastation.

The Global Nature of Modern Crises

The October 7th attacks and their global repercussions demonstrated the interconnected nature of our world. What began as a localized conflict quickly became a global crisis, affecting everything from international diplomacy to oil prices to community relations in cities thousands of miles from the Middle East.

Trey explored this theme in a series of reports titled "The Global Ripples of October 7th." He traveled to various countries, documenting how the crisis was impacting communities worldwide. In one segment, filmed in a diverse neighborhood in London, Trey observed:

"What happens in Gaza or Jerusalem doesn't stay there. It ripples out, affecting relationships between communities across the globe. Understanding this interconnectedness is crucial if we're to address the root causes of conflict and build a more peaceful world."

This perspective highlighted the need for global citizenship education and a more inclusive approach to addressing international challenges.

The Power and Responsibility of Information

Finally, the October 7th crisis underscored both the power of information to shape perceptions and drive action, and the responsibility that comes with that power. The rapid spread of both accurate reporting and misinformation in the wake of the attacks demonstrated the critical role that an informed citizenry plays in shaping responses to global events. Trey became an advocate for media literacy education, arguing that in the digital age, the ability to critically evaluate information is as important as traditional literacy. In a TED Talk given six months after the attacks, he said:

"What we choose to believe, share, and act upon shapes our world. The events of October 7th and their aftermath showed us that information can be a tool for understanding and healing, or a weapon that deepens divides. The choice is ours, and it's a responsibility we all share."

This call to action resonated with educators and policymakers, leading to increased emphasis on media literacy in school curricula and public education campaigns.

As Trey Yingst continued to report on the long-term impacts of October 7th, these lessons remained at the forefront of his work. They informed not just his approach to journalism, but his understanding of the world and his role in it. Through his reporting, writing, and advocacy, Trey worked to ensure that the hard-won insights from this tragedy would contribute to a more informed, compassionate, and resilient global community.

The story of October 7th, 2023 – the Saturday that turned black – was far from over. Its repercussions would continue to shape lives, policies, and global dynamics for years to come. But through the lessons learned and the stories told, there emerged a hope that from even the darkest days, humanity could find a path toward greater understanding, resilience, and ultimately, peace.

Conclusion

The Continuing Story: Israel, Palestine, and the Quest for Peace

As the dust settled on the immediate aftermath of October 7th, 2023, the long-standing conflict between Israel and Palestine entered a new, uncertain phase. The scars left by that fateful day ran deep, reshaping the political landscape and challenging long-held assumptions about the path to peace in the region.

In the months and years that followed, the quest for a lasting resolution to the Israeli-Palestinian conflict took on a renewed urgency. The horror of October 7th served as a reminder of the human cost of continued hostility, spurring international efforts to revive the peace process.

However, the road ahead proved to be as challenging as ever. The trauma inflicted on both sides hardened positions and deepened mistrust. In Israel, the security breach on October 7th led to a shift towards more hawkish policies, with increased emphasis on military solutions and border security. The Palestinian territories, meanwhile, grappled with the devastating aftermath of Israel's retaliatory actions in Gaza, fueling resentment and despair among the population.

Yet, amidst the darkness, glimmers of hope emerged. Grassroots peace initiatives, often led by those who had suffered personal losses in the conflict, gained traction. These efforts, while small in scale, demonstrated the enduring human desire for coexistence and reconciliation.

International mediators, learning from past failures, adopted new approaches to peace-building. There was a growing recognition that any lasting solution would need to address not just political boundaries, but economic disparities, access to resources, and the psychological wounds inflicted by decades of conflict.

The Abraham Accords faced their most significant test in the wake of October 7th. While the immediate reaction was one of shock and potential retrenchment, the long-term impact was more nuanced. Some argued that the crisis underscored the need for regional cooperation, potentially opening new avenues for dialogue and mediation.

As the years passed, the story of Israel and Palestine continued to evolve. New leaders emerged, shaped by the events of October 7th but not beholden to old narratives. Technological advancements offered novel solutions to long-standing issues, from water scarcity to border security. The global community, increasingly interconnected, found new ways to engage with and influence the peace process.

Yet, for all the changes, the fundamental issues at the heart of the conflict remained. The quest for security, dignity, and self-determination continued to drive both Israelis and Palestinians. The memory of October 7th, while slowly receding into history, remained a powerful reminder of the stakes involved in finding a peaceful resolution.

In this ongoing story, journalism played a crucial role. Reporters like Trey Yingst, who had witnessed the horrors of October 7th firsthand, continued to bring the realities of the conflict to a global audience. Their work ensured that the world remained engaged with the Israeli-Palestinian issue, preventing it from fading into the background of international attention.

The path to peace in Israel and Palestine remained long and fraught with challenges. But as long as there were those willing to tell the story, to bear witness to both the tragedies and the triumphs, hope remained alive. The quest for peace, though often seeming impossible, continued – a testament to the resilience of the human spirit and the enduring belief in a better future.

As this biography comes to a close, Trey Yingst's story is far from over. His journey, like the ongoing quest for peace in the Middle East, continues. With each report filed, each story told, he honors the memories of those affected by October 7th and contributes to the global understanding of conflict, resilience, and the enduring hope for peace.

In Trey's own words, from a recent interview: "October 7th changed me forever. It showed me the worst of humanity, but also the best. It taught me that even in the darkest moments, there are stories of hope and courage waiting to be told. As long as there are people working for peace, struggling to rebuild their lives, and believing in a better future,

I'll be there to tell their stories. That's not just my job – it's my calling."

And so, Trey Yingst moves forward, carrying with him the lessons of October 7th, continuing to bear witness to the world's conflicts and triumphs, one story at a time.

Acknowledgments

Writing this book has been a journey that parallels the events it describes – challenging, enlightening, and ultimately transformative. It would not have been possible without the support, guidance, and contributions of many individuals to whom I owe a debt of gratitude.

First and foremost, I must thank Trey Yingst for his openness, honesty, and willingness to revisit some of the most difficult moments of his career. Trey's commitment to truth-telling and his deep empathy for those affected by the events of October 7th shine through in every page of this book. His courage in sharing not just his experiences, but also his personal reflections and emotional journey, has made this biography far richer than I could have imagined.

To Jake and Mira, Trey's steadfast companions during the October 7th coverage, I extend my heartfelt thanks. Your insights into the challenges of reporting from conflict zones and your personal recollections of those harrowing days added invaluable depth to this narrative.

I am deeply grateful to the many individuals who shared their stories – survivors of the October 7th attacks, families of victims, first responders, and community leaders. Your bravery in reliving those traumatic events for the sake of this book is truly humbling. Your stories are the heart of this work, and I hope I have done justice to your experiences.

To the journalists, diplomats, and experts who provided context and analysis for this book, thank you for your time and expertise. Your insights helped frame the events of October 7th within the broader historical and geopolitical context, enriching the reader's understanding of this complex situation.

I owe a special debt of gratitude to my editor, Sarah, whose keen eye and insightful feedback helped shape this manuscript into its final form. Your ability to see the bigger picture while attending to the smallest details has elevated this work immeasurably.

To my research assistant, Alex, thank you for your tireless efforts in fact-checking, sourcing images, and tracking down elusive pieces of information. Your attention to detail and commitment to accuracy have been invaluable.

I am profoundly grateful to my family for their support throughout the writing process. To my parents, who instilled in me a love of storytelling and a deep respect for journalism, thank you for always believing in me and supporting my career choices.

Finally, I want to express my gratitude to the readers who have chosen to engage with this difficult but important story. Your willingness to bear witness to these events, to contend with their implications, and to consider their lessons for the future gives meaning to the work of journalists like Trey Yingst and authors like myself.

This book is dedicated to all those affected by the events of October 7th, 2023 – may their stories serve as a reminder of the human cost of conflict and the enduring hope for peace.

The End.

Made in the USA
Columbia, SC
10 October 2024

44077838R00126